big book of
gardendesigns

Marianne Lipanovich and Tom Wilhite

SUNSET BOOKS, MENLO PARK, CALIFORNIA

contents

introduction | 4

design ideas | 8

SUNSET BOOKS

VICE PRESIDENT, EDITORIAL DIRECTOR:
    Bob Doyle
DIRECTOR OF SALES: Brad Moses
DIRECTOR OF OPERATIONS: Rosann
    Sutherland
MARKETING MANAGER: Linda Barker
ART DIRECTOR: Vasken Guiragossian

STAFF FOR THIS BOOK

MANAGING EDITOR: Marianne Lipanovich
CONSULTING EDITOR: Tom Wilhite
ART DIRECTOR: Alice Rogers
COPY EDITOR/INDEXER: Barbara J. Braasch
PREPRESS COORDINATOR: Eligio Hernández
PRODUCTION SPECIALIST: Linda M. Bouchard
PRODUCTION ASSISTANTS: Susan Paris, Janis Reed
MAP DESIGN AND PRODUCTION:
    Reineck & Reineck, San Francisco
PROOFREADERS: Joan Erickson, Danielle Johnson

COVER PHOTOGRAPH: Rob D. Brodman
GARDEN DESIGN: Samantha Dardick Mier and
    Joel Mier in collaboration with Jon Buerk,
    J. Buerk Landscape/Maintenance

10 9 8 7 6 5 4 3
First Printing January 2008
Copyright © 2008, Sunset Publishing Corporation,
Menlo Park, CA 94025. First edition.

For additional copies of *Big Book of Garden
Designs* or any other Sunset book, visit us at
www.sunsetbooks.com.

For more exciting home and garden ideas, visit
myhomeîdeas.com

The Big Book of Garden Designs is organized into two main sections. "Design Ideas" provides a space-by-space look at designs for every area in your landscape. "Themes and Variations" focuses on designs for specialty gardens, such as theme gardens, color gardens, vegetable and herb gardens, and gardens that attract wildlife. Finally, the "Climate Zones" section explains the Sunset Climate Zones, which will help you determine which plans will work for where you garden.

themes | 118
and variations

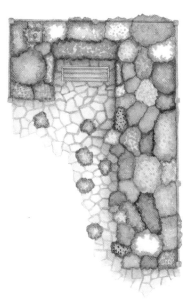

climate zones | 182

gardens by design

Why do some gardens "work"? The secret is in the planning. No matter how casual the look, creating an underlying plan is key to having a result that is appealing and just the garden you always wanted.

But all too often, novice gardeners—and even some experienced ones—feel intimidated by a bare patch of earth. The desire, of course, is to fill it with plants that

will look beautiful. The insecurity stems from trying to choose and arrange the right plants for the purpose. What will prosper? What will look good? Which plants will "go" together?

That's where this book steps in. The garden plans that follow are designed to meet all sorts of needs and please all styles of gardeners. You'll soon realize that

advance planning doesn't have to dictate hours
at the drawing board with a T square and triangle.
Some plans are very precise; others are more free
form. There are plans designed to fill an entire space,
whether it's small or large, but many more that are
designed to fit within a larger garden framework,
addressing typical landscape problem and situations—
and garden wish lists, too.

Many of these plans are designed to handle land-
scaping challenges common to virtually every garden.
Whether it's finding a good entry design, dealing with
tricky paths and side yards, filling in a garden bed, or
tackling a large backyard, you'll find plenty of ideas
on pages 8 through 117.

The plans on pages 118 through 181 are more
specialized. This is where you'll find ideas for creating
those one-of-a-kind spaces, such as a personal retreat,
a tropical paradise, a three-season cutting garden, a
flower/vegetable combination garden, a rock garden,
an alpine-inspired niche, or a display of succulents.
You'll also find ideas for single-color gardens and
those that feature a bold mix of colors.

Because no two houses are exactly alike, and even
more importantly, no two gardeners want exactly
the same thing, you'll find lots of variations in garden
styles and recommended plants. Many designs will
suit a wide range of climate zones; others focus on
particular regions with special gardening advantages
or limitations. The plans all include the climate zones

where the plants listed will thrive. To learn where your area fits in the Sunset's climate zone scheme, see pages 182 through 190.

Throughout this book you will also find featured Garden Closeups. The photos on these pages give you a closer look at how a particular garden works overall, providing ideas for designs and plantings to incorporate in your own space.

A second feature is the Designer Notebook. Landscape designer and author Tom Wilhite points out how the design elements in specific gardens make each space work. Consider these short seminars in good landscape design, and see how Tom's ideas can work for your own space.

Regardless of size or style, all of these plans aim to show you how to develop pleasing designs through effective plant combinations. And all are adaptable. You can use them as blueprints or as points of departure: replicate them exactly or just let them suggest lovely combinations you can adjust to your particular needs. The result will be your perfect garden.

reading the plans

For each design in this book, a photograph or illustration depicts the planting in its peak season. Accompanying each of these is a plot plan that shows the entire planted area. Within the plan, the area occupied by each type of plant is shaded in the basic color of its foliage or flowers and labeled with a letter. These letters correspond to those in the accompanying plant list, where the plants used are listed by botanical name and common name (if there is one). The total number of each plant needed for the plan is indicated in parentheses (for certain ground-cover plants typically sold by the flat, we do not give a number). To see where a plant fits into the design, check for its letter on the plan. The example shown is taken from pages 78–79.

PLAN ILLUSTRATION AND DESCRIPTION

A PERENNIAL SOLO A border composed entirely of perennials provides a spectacular display. This border contains five different perennials and a total of 13 plants. All are easy to grow, with blooms that will last for many weeks. These plants do well in Zones 2–10, 14–24, 30, 32–33, 37, 39.

PLOT PLAN

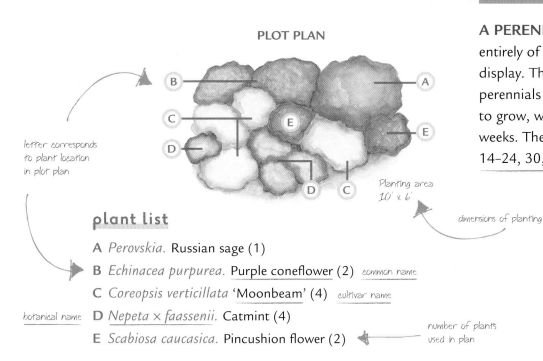

letter corresponds to plant location in plot plan

Planting area 10' x 6'

dimensions of planting

climate zones suitable for planting (see pages 182-190)

plant list

A *Perovskia.* Russian sage (1)

B *Echinacea purpurea.* Purple coneflower (2)   common name

C *Coreopsis verticillata* 'Moonbeam' (4)   cultivar name

botanical name   D *Nepeta* × *faassenii.* Catmint (4)

E *Scabiosa caucasica.* Pincushion flower (2)

number of plants used in plan

design ideas
garden by garden

first impressions ◊ sitting spots ◊ passageways
beds and borders ◊ backyards

A red gate, with contrasting blue-gray posts, is a natural focal point in this inviting entry garden. A wide path, paved with warm-hued bricks, emphasizes the balance and symmetry of the garden itself. Lush plantings of annuals, perennials, and shrubs soften the path's edges while showcasing some of the homeowner's favorite plants.

first impressions

Creating a good first impression is important. That short trip from public space to private front door offers the first glimpse of your domain. An unadorned concrete ribbon that takes dead aim from sidewalk to door, bisecting a lawn on the way, is not very inspiring to your guests or uplifting for you. Why not chart a more imaginative course? Gently curving paths, beds of flowers, trees and shrubs that complement your home's architectural style are all elements that can turn a bland entry into something special.

At the same time, a well-designed entry can also provide a degree of privacy that can't be found in a vast expanse of lawn and concrete. Carefully chosen plants incorporated into a pleasing garden design can help screen your windows from casual passersby without blocking the light—or the view from inside your home.

The designs on the following 20 pages present a variety of appealing entry plantings; all can be adapted to existing situations or created from scratch if you're remodeling a landscape or moving into a new home. Look at them for the ideas; adapt them to fit your own personal needs and desires.

Sometimes less is more. Two small trees, placed in carefully chosen containers, complement rather than distract from the strong architectural details of this distinctive entry patio.

plant list

A *Rosa* 'Charisma' (standard) (2)

B *Gaillardia × grandiflora* 'Burgundy'. Blanket flower (1)

C *Rosa* 'Starina' (miniature) (5)

D *Dahlia* (orange) (2)

E *Limonium perezii.* Sea lavender (1)

F *Lavandula × intermedia* 'Provence'. Lavandin (2)

G *Lantana* 'Cream Carpet' (1)

H *Anigozanthos* 'Bush Gold'. Kangaroo paw (1)

I *Pelargonium × hortorum.* Common geranium (pink) (2)

J *Agave americana* 'Marginata'. Century plant (1)

K *Pelargonium crispum.* Lemon geranium (1)

L *Salvia elegans.* Pineapple sage (1)

M *Citrus* (dwarf) (1)

N *Pelargonium* 'Atomic Snowflake'. Scented geranium (1)

O *Rosa* 'Firefighter' (1)

P *Vinca major.* Periwinkle (1)

Q *Rosa* 'Sunset Celebration' (1)

R *Achillea × taygetea.* Yarrow (1)

S *Buxus sempervirens.* Common boxwood (hedge)

T *Lobularia maritima.* Sweet alyssum (2)

A FRAGRANT WELCOME A container garden that focuses on color and fragrance offers a gracious welcome to guests and to the family that lives here. Matching planters at the bottom of the steps and on each side of the door provide a touch of formality that echoes the style of the house. In between the two, a mix of complementary plants and planters keeps the look fresh and interesting. The plants shown here do well in Zones 15–24, but the design ideas can be repeated in any climate.

Patio area *12' × 8'*

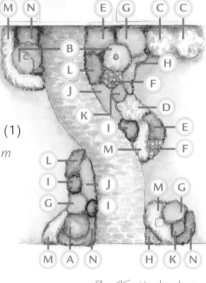

Plan 25' wide along house

FREE-FORM CURVES

Surprising though it may seem, the natural walking path between two unobstructed points is not a straight line but a gently sinuous curve. Here, such a route gives the approach the feel of a relaxed amble rather than a no-time-to-spare rush. The plan works best where it gets just a touch of shade (as from high, open trees) during the afternoon. It's most successful in Zones 4–6, 32, 34, 37, and 39, but you can also enjoy it in Zones 3, 35, 36, 38, 40, and 41 by using *Rhododendron (azalea)* 'Orchid Lights' in place of *R. mucronulatum* 'Cornell Pink' (B in the list at right) and replacing *R.* 'Boule de Neige' (C) with *Hydrangea arborescens* 'Annabelle'.

plant list

A *Acer palmatum* 'Ornatum'. Red laceleaf Japanese maple (1)

B *Rhododendron mucronulatum* 'Cornell Pink' (2)

C *Rhododendron* 'Boule de Neige' (2+)

D *Daphne × burkwoodii* 'Carol Mackie' (1)

E *Helleborus niger.* Christmas rose (6)

F *Astrantia major.* Masterwort (3)

G *Alchemilla mollis.* Lady's-mantle (7)

H *Heuchera micrantha* 'Palace Purple'. Coral bells (7)

I *Bergenia* 'Bressingham Ruby' (5)

J *Astilbe simplicifolia* 'Sprite'. False spirea (9)

K *Hosta* 'Krossa Regal'. Plantain lily (2)

L *Hosta tardiflora.* Plantain lily (9)

M *Hakonechloa macra* 'Aureola'. Japanese forest grass (16)

N *Ajuga reptans.* Carpet bugle (18+)

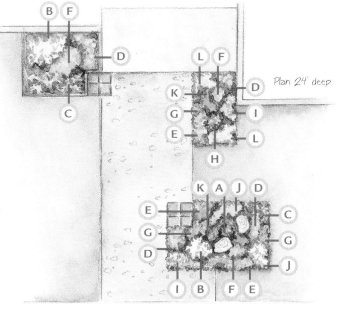

DIRECT ACCESS No doubt about it: this path gets you to the front door in a straight line. Yet the walkway also forms part of a larger design with the three rectangular beds that flank and intersect it. Suited to mild-winter California and the arid Southwest (Zones 8, 9, 12–24), the planting appears lush, but all its members require just moderate watering. Floral color is at its height in spring, before the inevitable heat in many of the zones noted above slows or stops growth for the summer.

plant list

A *Phormium* 'Maori Chief' (1)

B *Cistus* 'Doris Hibberson'. Rockrose (2)

C *Cistus* 'Warley Rose'. Rockrose (3)

D *Convolvulus cneorum.* Bush morning glory (8)

E *Convolvulus sabatius.* Ground morning glory (6)

F *Euphorbia × martinii* (5)

G *Aloe maculata* (5)

H *Phormium tenax* 'Bronze Baby'. New Zealand flax (1)

I *Osteospermum fruticosum.* Trailing African daisy (6)

J *Oenothera speciosa.* Mexican evening primrose (8)

K *Teucrium × lucidrys* 'Prostratum'. Germander (8)

L *Zinnia grandiflora* (6)

plant list

A *Hamamelis × intermedia* 'Ruby Glow'. Witch hazel (1)

B *Magnolia* 'Betty' (1)

C *Enkianthus campanulatus* (1)

D *Pinus mugo*. Mugho pine (1)

E *Rhododendron yakushimanum* 'Koichiro Wada' (2)

F *Erica × darleyensis* 'Silberschmelze'. Heath (5)

G *Erica* 'Dawn'. Heath (7)

H *Calluna vulgaris* 'Nana'. Heather (6)

I *Viburnum davidii* (2)

J *Juniperus rigida conferta*. Shore juniper (3)

K *Epimedium × versicolor* 'Sulphureum' (11)

L *Helleborus orientalis*. Lenten rose (9)

M *Heuchera micrantha* 'Palace Purple'. Coral bells (16)

N *Imperata cylindrica* 'Rubra'. Japanese blood grass (10)

O *Campanula portenschlagiana*. Dalmatian bellflower (9)

P *Sagina subulata* 'Aurea'. Scotch moss (eighteen to twenty 3-inch squares, spaced 6 inches apart)

Q *Ajuga reptans*. Carpet bugle (15)

R *Rhododendron (azalea)* 'Coral Bells' (2)

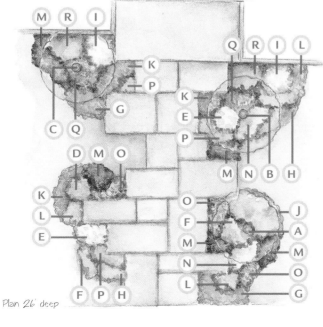

Plan 26' deep

DIVERSIONARY TACTIC Deliberate asymmetry disguises the fact that this entry path actually moves directly from sidewalk to front door. Rectangular pavers of different sizes are laid out in a staggered pattern, their edges softened with irregularly shaped planting beds. Suitable for Pacific Northwest Zones 4–6 and coastal California Zones 15–17, this scheme offers year-round visual interest. The blossoms on shrubs and perennials come and go from midwinter through fall, while the foliage of perennials and low shrubs offers sustained color. In winter, the bare limbs of deciduous shrubs serve as living sculpture.

plant list

A *Stachys byzantina.* Lamb's ears (10)

B *Rudbeckia hirta.* Black-eyed Susan (1)

C *Hemerocallis,* red and orange hybrids. Daylily (3)

D *Solidago.* Goldenrod (10)

E *Caryopteris × clandonensis.* Blue mist. (4)

F *Buddleja davidii* 'Black Knight'. Butterfly bush (1)

G *Calamagrostis × acutiflora* 'Karl Foerster'. Feather reed grass (4)

H *Cercocarpus ledifolius.* Curl-leaf mountain mahogany (1)

I *Tithonia rotundifolia.* Mexican sunflower (6)

J *Perovskia.* Russian sage (2)

K *Miscanthus sinensis.* Eulalia, Japanese silver grass (1)

L *Penstemon* Mexicali hybrid 'Pike's Peak Purple' (3)

M *Spiraea trilobata* 'Fairy Queen'. Spirea (4)

N *Lavandula angustifolia.* English lavender (3)

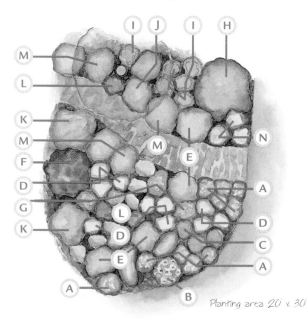

Planting area 20' × 30'

LUSH LOOK Colorful but unthirsty plants make up this lush-looking entry garden. These plants thrive in the windy, sun-drenched climate of Colorado Springs, though they will do well in any sunny spot in Zones 2–9, 14–21. Soft, silvery lamb's ears, black-eyed Susans, and red daylilies flank the driveway, while goldenrod and blue mist spirea fill in the beds. Purple-flowered Black Knight butterfly bush and wheatlike feather reed grass add height and texture near the house, while a craggy ponderosa pine anchors a showy display of burnt-orange blooms of Mexican sunflowers and lavender Russian sage.

FRANKLY MODERN An essentially straight entry path and angular planting beds reinforce the stripped-down, no-frills architecture of the 1950s. Yet the beds also relieve the rigidity: because they impinge on either side of the walk, the journey to the front door describes a gentle curve. Many of the plants are mounding or billowy, softening the straight lines of walk and bed edges—but the fortnight lily, phormium, and daylily offer spiky and fountainlike foliage clumps as well. Flowering starts in spring, with most perennials continuing through summer. Use this plan in full sun, in Zones 8, 9, 14–24.

plant list

A *Nandina domestica.* Heavenly bamboo (1)

B *Rhaphiolepis indica* 'Indian Princess'. Indian hawthorn (5+)

C *Berberis thunbergii* 'Crimson Pygmy'. Japanese barberry (2)

D *Phormium* 'Apricot Queen' (1)

E *Dietes bicolor.* Fortnight lily (1)

F *Hemerocallis* 'Stella de Oro'. Daylily (2)

G *Salvia officinalis* 'Berggarten'. Common sage (3)

H *Achillea millefolium,* Galaxy strain. Common yarrow (4)

I *Limonium platyphyllum.* Sea lavender (7)

J *Iberis sempervirens* 'Snowflake'. Evergreen candytuft (6)

K *Verbena* 'Tapien Purple'. Moss verbena (8)

L *Teucrium* × *lucidrys* 'Prostratum'. Germander (10)

M *Cerastium tomentosum.* Snow-in-summer (6)

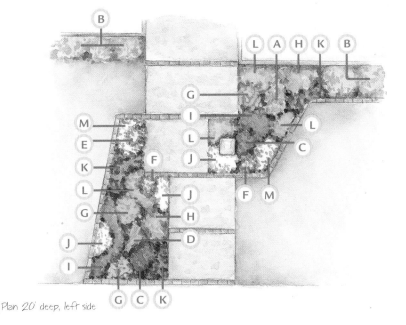

Plan 20' deep, left side

A FRONT YARD "SECRET GARDEN"

Why welcome friends and family to your home with just grass or a ground cover when you can wow them with an ever-changing tapestry of foliage and flowers? If your entry area is small, you can easily plant this garden in the plot bounded by sidewalk, driveway, and entry walk. Here, the addition of a post-and-rail fence provides a subtle foil for the plantings that flank and flow through it, adding a sense of secrecy. All the plants thrive in Zones 4–9, 14–24.

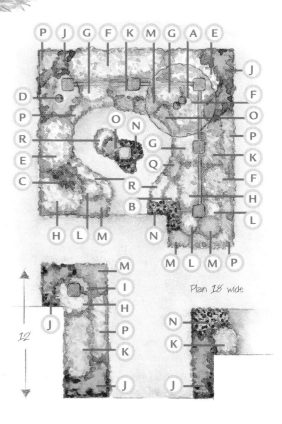

Plan 18' wide

plant list

A *Cercis occidentalis.*
Western redbud (1)

B *Calamagrostis × acutiflora* 'Karl Foerster'.
Feather reed grass (1)

C *Chaenomeles* 'Enchantress'.
Flowering quince (1)

D *Rhamnus alaternus* 'Variegata'.
Italian buckthorn (1)

E *Teucrium fruticans.*
Bush germander (5)

F *Abelia × grandiflora* 'Edward Goucher'.
Glossy abelia (5)

G *Lavandula angustifolia.*
English lavender (3)

H *Achillea millefolium,* Galaxy strain.
Common yarrow (10)

I *Lonicera × heckrottii.*
Goldflame honeysuckle (1)

J *Mahonia aquifolium* 'Compacta'.
Oregon grape (16)

K *Spiraea japonica* 'Goldflame'. Spirea (8)

L *Euphorbia characias wulfenii* (3)

M *Salvia officinalis* 'Berggarten'.
Common sage (8)

N *Verbena* 'Tapien Purple'. Moss verbena (12)

O *Hemerocallis,* apricot pink cultivar.
Daylily (4)

P *Liriope spicata.* Creeping lily turf (22)

Q *Sedum* 'Autumn Joy'. Stonecrop (4)

R *Coreopsis verticillata* 'Moonbeam' (8)

plant list

A *Buddleja davidii* 'Black Knight'. Butterfly bush (1)

B *Buddleja* 'Lochinch'. Butterfly bush (1)

C *Phlomis russeliana* (4+)

D *Miscanthus sinensis* 'Purpurascens'. Eulalia, Japanese silver grass (1)

E *Pennisetum alopecuroides* 'Hameln'. Fountain grass (2)

F *Achillea* 'Fireland'. Yarrow (2)

G *Achillea filipendulina* 'Coronation Gold'. Fernleaf yarrow (4)

H *Achillea* 'Moonshine'. Yarrow (10)

I *Hemerocallis* 'Happy Returns' or other short yellow. Daylily (5)

J *Sedum* 'Autumn Joy'. Stonecrop (9)

K *Salvia* × *sylvestris* 'May Night'. Sage (11)

L *Chrysanthemum weyrichii* 'White Bomb' (10)

M *Artemisia stelleriana* 'Silver Brocade'. Beach wormwood (17)

FRAMED BY IRREGULAR BEDS

Even if a perfectly straight entry walk is the best choice for your landscape, it doesn't have to look like a package ribbon tied across the yard. Here, curving beds hold relaxed plantings of shrubs and perennials, arranged in outward-sweeping drifts that de-emphasize the underlying severity. Leaf shapes vary, but all the plants are mounding, billowing, or spreading, offering a soft contrast to the straight walk. Warm flower colors play against cooler hues of white, silver, blue, and violet.

This plan is suited to Zones 3–6, 31, 32, 34, 35, 37, 39. To extend it to Zones 2, 40, and 41, replace A, B, C, and E in the list below with (respectively): beauty bush (*Kolkwitzia amabilis*); *Weigela* hybrid 'Variegata'; *Spiraea japonica* 'Goldmound'; and variegated purple moor grass (*Molinia caerulea* 'Variegata').

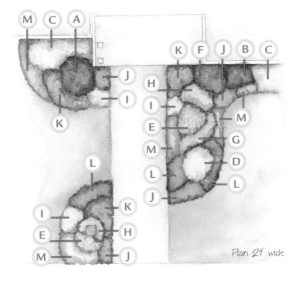

Plan 29' wide

A FLOWERY WELCOME Whether your front yard is spacious or small, you can dazzle your visitors and satisfy your gardening soul with plantings full of flowers.

If a driveway extends past the house to a garage farther back (as shown on this page), an entry walk can link drive and front door; the challenge here is to craft a planting striking enough to draw attention away from so much bare pavement.

In the plan below, especially fine in Zones 3–6, 32–41, a gently winding path is flanked by irregular beds that give three-season color from flowers and foliage, including some fall leaf color.

plant list

A *Acer palmatum* 'Sango Kaku'. Japanese maple (1)

B *Juniperus rigida conferta*. Shore juniper (4+)

C *Berberis thunbergii* 'Crimson Pygmy'. Japanese barberry (6)

D *Clematis* 'The President' (1)

E *Rosa* 'White Dawn' (1)

F *Clethra alnifolia*. Summersweet (1)

G *Viburnum opulus* 'Compactum'. European cranberry bush (2)

H *Spiraea japonica* 'Goldflame'. Spirea (2)

I *Chrysanthemum pacificum*. Gold and silver chrysanthemum (4)

J *Molinia caerulea* 'Variegata'. Variegated purple moor grass (2)

K *Achillea* 'Fireland'. Yarrow (4)

L *Iris*, Siberian, 'Fourfold White' (4)

M *Hemerocallis* 'Happy Returns' or other short yellow cultivar. Daylily (9)

N *Rudbeckia fulgida sullivantii* 'Goldsturm' (3)

O *Salvia* × *sylvestris* 'May Night'. Sage (16)

P *Sedum* 'Autumn Joy'. Stonecrop (7)

Q *Prunella grandiflora*. Self-heal (28)

If your front yard is shallow, planting this design with just a small lawn may make the space seem overexposed to the street. Add the illusion of depth by converting the entire yard to garden (as shown on this page), with converging paths from drive and sidewalk leading through a three-season flower fête. This scheme suits California Zones 8, 9, 14–24, where new homes are being built on ever smaller lots.

plant list

A *Lagerstroemia* 'Natchez' (multitrunked). Crape myrtle (1)

B *Rosa,* such as 'First Light', 'Iceberg', 'Scentimental' (4)

C *Rosa* 'The Fairy', as standard (1)

D *Coleonema album.* White breath of heaven (3)

E *Escallonia* 'Apple Blossom' (1)

F *Artemisia* 'Powis Castle' (6)

G *Erigeron karvinskianus.* Santa Barbara daisy (7)

H *Penstemon* 'Firebird'. Border penstemon (4)

I *Nepeta* × *faassenii.* Catmint (6)

J *Erysimum* 'Bowles Mauve'. Wallflower (7)

K *Achillea millefolium* 'Appleblossom'. Common yarrow (3)

L *Calamagrostis* × *acutiflora* 'Karl Foerster'. Feather reed grass (2)

M *Thymus praecox arcticus.* Mother-of-thyme (17)

N *Stachys byzantina* 'Silver Carpet'. Lamb's ears (9)

O *Geranium sanguineum.* Bloody cranesbill (3)

P *Festuca trachyphylla.* Sheep's fescue (21)

Q *Liriope muscari* 'Silvery Sunproof'. Big blue lily turf (12)

R *Potentilla neumanniana.* Cinquefoil (40)

S *Mahonia aquifolium* 'Compacta'. Oregon grape (12)

Island 26' wide

front yard serenity | on the right path

Wide flagstone slabs, a mix of shrubs, and a richly textured garden filled with ornamental grasses, ground covers, and Japanese maples create a tranquil entry to this home. The hostas, maples, and Japanese forest grass thrive in this shady location, and the rugged, in-scale boulders on either side of the walk give the look of a placid stream flowing through a natural landscape.

A specimen weeping Japanese maple is the spotlight planting in this raised berm that sits alongside the entry walk. Japanese forest grass, hostas, and baby tears planted around the base provide a soft setting while allowing a good view of the maple's delicate branches and weeping habit.

A terra-cotta urn is tucked among the gold-spotted leaves of the aucuba and spiky foliage of lily turf, glowing serenely in a quiet, light-filled corner near the front door. The decorative ironwork panel serves as a backdrop.

plant list

A *Acer palmatum.* Japanese maple

B *Echeveria × imbricata.* Hen and chicks

C *Aucuba japonica.* Japanese aucuba

D *Lamium maculatum.* Dead nettle

E *Hakonechloa macra* 'Aureola'. Japanese forest grass

F *Hosta* 'Golden Tiara'. Plantain lily

G *Liriope gigantea.* Lily turf

H *Soleirolia soleirolii.* Baby's tears (as underplanting)

I *Viola labradorica.* Viola

J *Prunus caroliniana.* Carolina laurel cherry

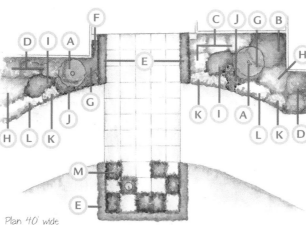

GRAND ENTRANCE In bygone days, a curving drive was a standard feature of wealthy homes, typically sweeping under a porte cochere where elegant carriages paused to discharge their occupants. Today, such drives usually lack the imposing overhead and are likely to serve only ordinary vehicles. Still, this design retains a bit of yesteryear's formality. Color appears in all seasons, but aside from the striking display provided by azaleas and Indian hawthorn, the amount at any given moment is restrained. The sweet olive's blossoms, in fact, proclaim their presence by their penetrating fragrance. All the plants are evergreen, appropriate for Western and Southeastern Zones 14–24, 28–31.

Plan 40' wide

plant list

A *Osmanthus fragrans.* Sweet olive (2)

B *Rhaphiolepis indica* 'Springtime'. Indian hawthorn (1)

C *Rhododendron (azalea)* 'Gumpo' (4)

D *Rhododendron (azalea)* 'Gumpo Pink' (5+)

E *Buxus microphylla koreana* 'Tide Hill'. Korean boxwood (33)

F *Camellia sasanqua* 'Mine-No-Yuki' ('White Doves') (1)

G *Liriope muscari* 'Silvery Sunproof'. Big blue lily turf (18)

H *Nandina domestica* 'Harbor Dwarf'. Heavenly bamboo (7)

I *Aspidistra elatior.* Cast-iron plant (8)

J *Ajuga reptans.* Carpet bugle (16)

K *Hemerocallis* 'Stella de Oro'. Daylily (5)

L *Iberis sempervirens* 'Snowflake'. Evergreen candytuft (11)

M *Ophiopogon japonicus.* Mondo grass (24)

GRAND ENTRANCE, COUNTRY STYLE In the country and suburban front yards, where land is more plentiful, the crescent drive offers an efficient entry for both cars and people. By running it through a garden, you make it interesting as well as practical. In this plan, the front yard could be shallow or quite deep. In either case, the low, open fence defines the planting while still letting parts of it flow through to the "outside."

Gardeners in chilly Zones 2–6, 32–41 will appreciate the hardiness of these plants. Flowers come and go during spring and summer; woody plants give good fall leaf color and some showy fruits.

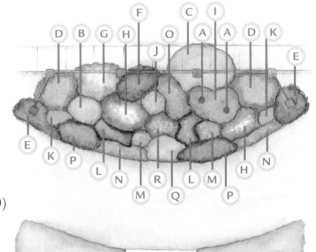

Planting area 40 x 12

plant list

A *Crataegus phaenopyrum.* Washington thorn (2)

B *Cornus alba* 'Elegantissima'. Tatarian dogwood (1)

C *Xanthorhiza simplicissima.* Yellowroot (3)

D *Rosa* 'Frau Dagmar Hartopp' ('Fru Dagmar Hastrup') (3)

E *Cotoneaster adpressus.* Creeping cotoneaster (7)

F *Berberis thunbergii* 'Atropurpurea'. Red-leaf Japanese barberry (2)

G *Lysimachia clethroides.* Gooseneck loosestrife (3)

H *Astilbe × arendsii* 'Bridal Veil'. False spirea (8)

I *Athyrium filix-femina.* Lady fern (7)

J *Iris,* Siberian, light blue cultivar (2)

K *Hemerocallis,* cream to light yellow cultivar. Daylily (4)

L *Epimedium × versicolor* 'Sulphureum' (9)

M *Bergenia* 'Abendglut' ('Evening Glow') or 'Bressingham Ruby' (3)

N *Hosta* 'Gold Edger'. Plantain lily (9)

O *Galium odoratum.* Sweet woodruff (7)

P *Thymus praecox arcticus* 'Coccineum'. Mother-of-thyme (20)

Q *Sagina subulata* 'Aurea'. Scotch moss (fifteen 3-inch squares, set 6 inches apart)

R *Chamaemelum nobile.* Chamomile (9)

Plan 24' wide

CONTEMPORARY GATED ENTRANCE

If privacy or noise abatement is a priority, a substantial wall with an entry gate is a good choice. With the wall set back from the street, the challenge is to come up with an attractive streetside planting that is uncluttered and easy to maintain. The focus is on the wall's public face. The overall design is formal—but the plants are largely informal, tied together by a tightly trimmed boxwood hedge. Foliage variegation and seasonal flowers on hydrangea and weigela, as well as blossoms on the magnolias, keep the planting looking interesting. This plan suits Zones 3–9, 14–17, 32–34, 39. To use it in Zones 2, 35–38, and 41, substitute Korean boxwood (*Buxus microphylla koreana*) and *Hydrangea arborescens* 'Annabelle' for the boxwood and hydrangea selections in the plant list.

plant list

A *Buxus microphylla japonica* 'Green Beauty'. Japanese boxwood (46+)

B *Hydrangea macrophylla* 'Tricolor'. Bigleaf hydrangea (2)

C *Magnolia kobus* 'Wada's Memory'. Kobus magnolia (2)

D *Weigela* hybrid 'Variegata' (4+)

plant list

A *Osteospermum fruticosum.* Trailing African daisy (3)

B *Agave americana* 'Striata'. Century plant (1)

C *Lavandula angustifoila.* English lavender (2)

D *Phormium* hybrids (3)

E *Origanum rotundifolium* 'Kent Beauty'. Oregano (1)

F *Armeria girardii.* Thrift (1)

G *Euphorbia* × *martinii* (1)

H *Verbena* hybrids (6)

I *Rosmarinus officinalis.* Rosemary (1)

J *Agapanthus* 'Peter Pan'. Lily-of-the-Nile (1)

K *Coleonema pulchellum.* Pink breath of heaven (1)

L *Daphne cneorum.* Garland daphne (1)

M *Armeria maritima.* Common thrift (3)

N *Achillea millefolium.* Common yarrow (1)

O *Thymus* × *citriodorus.* Lemon thyme (3)

P *Carex divulsa.* Berkeley sedge (1)

Q *Pelargonium.* Scented geraniums (4)

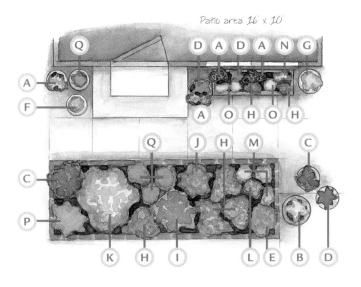

Patio area *16' x 10'*

GARDENER'S POT LUCK When an avid gardener was faced with a 4- by 12-foot planter and an aggregate walk leading to his front door as his only gardening space, he didn't let that stop him. The brick planter was turned into a sophisticated rock garden. Then a collection of glazed and unglazed pots became a showcase for dozens of plants. Browsing deer are a constant threat to the plant collection, but the phormium, a long-blooming hardy geranium, and fragrant thyme, oregano, and lavender have proved to be mostly deerproof. A striking variegated century plant, well armed with sharp spines, stands guard by the planter. This welcoming garden does well in Zones 14–17.

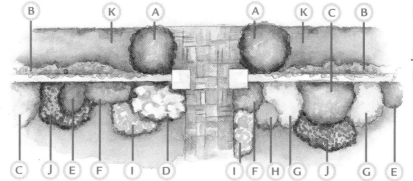

UNDERSTATED ELEGANCE A brick wall is the image of formality and restraint: when it separates public sidewalk from private yard, it clearly states "no trespassing." Nonetheless, its looks are often warm, not concrete-cold, conveying a welcome to those who are expected. In keeping with this reserved yet friendly mood, the plants in the scheme shown here are elegant without being formally stiff. Contrasts in foliage texture make a three-season statement; flower color is at its peak in late spring, with the hydrangea carrying on into summer. The lightest afternoon shade suits all these plants, which perform best in Zones 3–9, 14–17, 32–34, 37–39. To suit the plan to Zones 40 and 41, substitute *Hydrangea arborescens* 'Annabelle' and *Rhododendron (azalea)* 'Orchid Lights' for the hydrangea and rhododendron suggested at right under C and D.

Planting area: 40' x 11'

plant list

A *Berberis thunbergii* 'Cherry Bomb'. Japanese barberry (2)

B *Parthenocissus quinquefolia.* Virginia creeper (2)

C *Hydrangea serrata* 'Preziosa' (2)

D *Rhododendron yakushimanum* (2)

E *Iris,* Siberian, 'Caesar's Brother' (4)

F *Astrantia major.* Masterwort (6)

G *Alchemilla mollis.* Lady's-mantle (6)

H *Bergenia* 'Bressingham Ruby' (1)

I *Hosta* 'Gold Edger'. Plantain lily (9)

J *Epimedium alpinum* (7)

K *Pachysandra terminalis.* Japanese spurge (20+)

28

BEHIND THE WALL

Concrete paving and a stucco wall, a contemporary design approach with roots in Mediterranean antiquity, are hard, bright surfaces that look stark without the softening influence of plants—and the assortment shown here rises beautifully to the task. Mounded, irregular, loose, grassy, or frothy, they smooth sharp corners and gently blur straight edges. Summer is the prime flowering season in this garden. All the plants will succeed in Zones 3–7, 14–17, 32–34, 39. In Zones 35–38, 40, 41, you can substitute *Spiraea japonica* 'Goldmound' for phlomis (C in the list at right), *Verbena* 'Homestead Purple' for moss verbena (G), and catmint *(Nepeta × faassenii)* for germander (I).

Planting area 40' x 11'

plant list

A *Lonicera sempervirens.* Trumpet honeysuckle (2)
B *Caryopteris × clandonensis.* Blue mist (2)
C *Phlomis russeliana* (4+)
D *Panicum virgatum* 'Heavy Metal'. Switch grass (3)
E *Rudbeckia fulgida sullivantii* 'Goldsturm' (8)
F *Limonium platyphyllum.* Sea lavender (12+)
G *Verbena* 'Tapien Purple'. Moss verbena (18)
H *Cerastium tomentosum.* Snow-in-summer (16+)
I *Teucrium × lucidrys* 'Prostratum'. Germander (4)

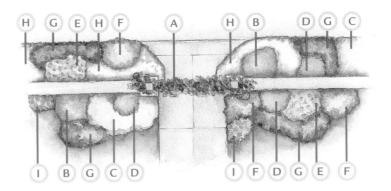

sculptural style

tom's notebook

Here's an entry garden ideally suited to the modern style of the house. The clean architectural lines make a great backdrop for large sculptural agaves and hedges of perfectly vertical horsetails. Set in a carpet of low-growing dymondia, bold rectangular pavers lead from the street to the sidewalk, and generously proportioned steps repeat the horizontal line. Grouped around the entry path are inviting, soft-looking blue fescue, Mexican feather grass, and orange New Zealand sedge.

The bench looks like a piece of minimalist sculpture, but situated in the shade of a spreading olive tree, it also offers a place to pause on the way to the front door. The garden's restrained hues of green, blue-gray, and buff are in perfect harmony with the house and allow the color focus to be on the dramatic shade of deep red used for the trim of the front door and the bench.

Tom

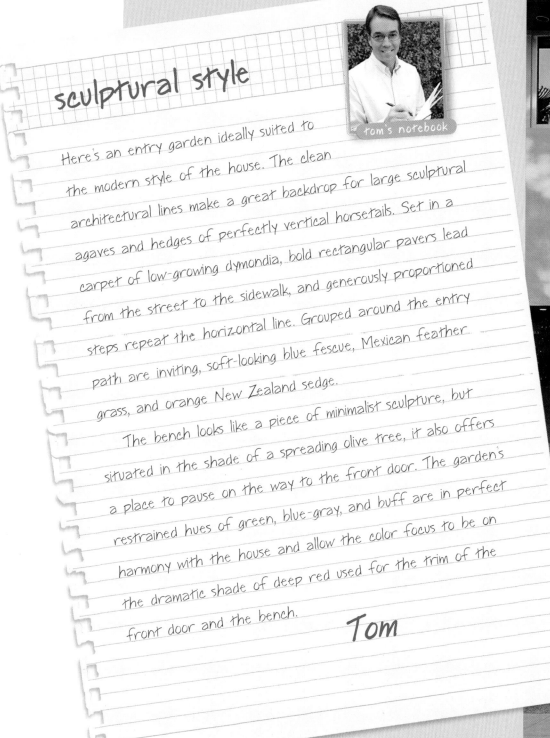

3

1 Blue-gray dymondia requires little care or water

2 Potentially invasive horsetail is contained by pavement

3 Low-maintenance senecio drapes attractively over wall

4 Olive tree is pruned up to reveal sculptural trunks

Contemporary meets tropical in this patio. Large pavers form the patio's base, highlighted by the bright blue tumbled glass that outlines each square. Brightly painted retaining walls and planters, set at differing heights, hold more plants and an above-ground water garden, while an angel's trumpet provides a bright yellow accent.

sitting spots

Patios, decks, and porches are the transition zones between your house and your garden. Whether you have a tiny apartment balcony or a multilevel deck overlooking a sprawling suburban landscape, the space offers plenty of gardening opportunities, and by playing up its role, you can end up with an area that is itself a garden destination. You can tie the plantings to a garden beyond, or create an oasis in a totally different style.

Pots and planters, the major players in any patio, porch, or deck design, are available in a multitude of sizes, which means you can plant tiny specimen plants to enjoy up close or larger shrubs and trees to create barriers and boundaries. The containers also allow you to move plants around until you get just the look you want—and to change plants that just aren't working.

Another advantage to these portable places is that you can go outside your climate zone. Tender plants can flourish outdoors and be brought inside when winters are cold; harsh sunlight can be more easily softened or eliminated to let you grow plants that prefer less heat and light.

The following pages offer ideas and suggestions for sprucing up plantings on and around patios and decks, and a closer look at how a plain porch can be turned into a garden.

Part path, part patio, this outdoor entertaining area nestles easily into the surrounding garden. The flagstone floor echoes the color of the stone wall, giving the space a cohesive feel.

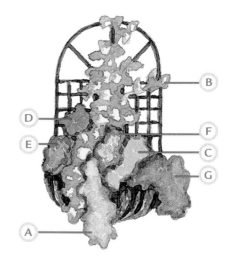

PATIO SHOWPLACE Plants in pots, plants in hanging planters, and plants nestled next to the bricks turn a simple brick patio into a garden retreat. Hanging planters and a star jasmine winding up a pole provide height, billowy edging plants soften the patio's hard edges, and groupings of pots showcase a succulent collection and bring the garden onto the patio itself. The garden is designed for Zones 14–24, but the container plants can be used as annuals in all zones.

wire basket plant list

A *Ipomoea batatas* 'Marguerite'. Sweet potato vine (1)

B *Thunbergia alata*. Black-eyed Susan vine (1)

C *Fuchsia × hybrida* (1)

D *Solenostemon scutellarioides*. Coleus (1)

E *Begonia semperflorens*. Wax begonia (1)

F *Heliotropium arborescens*. Common heliotrope (1)

G *Hedera helix* 'Hahn's Self Branching'. English ivy (1)

urn plant list

1 *Diascia* 'Coral Belle'. Twinspur (1)

2 *Carex elata* 'Knightshayes' (1)

3 *Helichrysum petiolare* 'Limelight'. Licorice plant (1)

4 *Nemesia caerulea* 'Blue Lagoon' (1)

plant list

A *Acer palmatum* 'Sango Kaku'. Japanese maple (1)

B *Cercis canadensis* 'Forest Pansy'. Eastern redbud (2)

C *Chaenomeles* 'Toyo Nishiki'. Flowering quince (1)

D *Clematis* 'Henryi' (2)

E *Rhododendron* 'Lem's Monarch' ('Pink Walloper') (1)

F *Rhododendron* 'Unique' (1)

G *Rhododendron* 'Moonstone' (1)

H *Rhododendron* 'PJM' (6)

I *Rhododendron (azalea)* 'Gumpo' (4)

J *Euonymus fortunei* 'Emerald Gaiety' (8)

K *Pieris japonica* 'Variegata'. Lily-of-the-valley shrub (3)

L *Calluna vulgaris* 'Blazeaway'. Scotch heather (5)

M *Hosta* 'Frances Williams'. Plantain lily (3)

N *Hosta* 'Hadspen Blue'. Plantain lily (4)

O *Iris foetidissima* 'Variegata'. Gladwin iris (2)

P *Helleborus orientalis*. Lenten rose (5)

Q *Sagina subulata* 'Aurea'. Scotch moss (3-inch squares, set 6 inches apart)

R *Pratia pedunculata*. Blue star creeper (twelve 3-inch squares, set 6 inches apart)

S *Equisetum hyemale*. Horsetail (1, in pot in pool)

KEEP IT SIMPLE Though this design calls for nineteen different plants, it gives the impression of unity and simplicity. Shrubs are its mainstay, and the mass planting of just a few sorts helps draw the garden together. Zones 4–6, 14–17 are best for this plan, but it will also succeed in Zones 34, 37, and 39 if you make a few changes: substitute locally successful rhododendrons and azaleas for those suggested under E through I in the list at right, use carpet bugle *(Ajuga reptans)* in place of blue star creeper (R), and eliminate the Gladwin iris (O).

Planting area 30' x 20'

SUMMER SHOWPIECE

Jam-packed with color, this jewel-like planting is a mere 20 feet deep and 30 feet wide. Stroll along the path that leads throughout the garden, pausing to admire each plant; or, for prolonged contemplation, take advantage of a sheltered gazebo or plein air bench. The planting is designed for chilly-winter Zones 3–6, 32–41, where summer is the prime season for floral splendor and outdoor living. The flowering year, though, begins in spring, with the early show of serviceberry, wisteria, plum, and lily-of-the-valley followed by the later spring blossoms of cranberry bush, mountain laurel, and Siberian iris.

plant list

A *Amelanchier × grandiflora.* Serviceberry (1)

B *Wisteria sinensis.* Chinese wisteria (1)

C *Prunus × cistena.* Dwarf red-leaf plum (2)

D *Viburnum opulus* 'Compactum'. European cranberry bush (2)

E *Kalmia latifolia.* Mountain laurel (2)

F *Kalmia latifolia* 'Elf'. Mountain laurel (2)

G *Spiraea japonica* 'Goldflame'. Spirea (4)

H *Spiraea japonica* 'Shirobana'. Spirea (3)

I *Berberis thunbergii.* Japanese barberry (4)

J *Berberis thunbergii* 'Crimson Pygmy'. Japanese barberry (1)

K *Potentilla fruticosa* 'Abbotswood'. Cinquefoil (3)

L *Calamagrostis × acutiflora* 'Karl Foerster'. Feather reed grass (1)

M *Gypsophila paniculata* 'Bristol Fairy'. Baby's breath (3)

N *Geranium himalayense* 'Plenum' (8)

O *Coreopsis verticillata* 'Moonbeam' (4)

P *Penstemon digitalis* 'Husker Red'. Beard tongue (4)

Q *Iris*, Siberian, blue cultivar (e.g. 'Orville Fay') (4)

R *Heuchera micrantha*. 'Palace Purple'. Coral bells (7)

S *Nepeta × faassenii.* Catmint (4)

T *Prunella grandiflora.* Self-heal (16)

U *Campanula portenschlagiana.* Dalmatian bellflower (5)

V *Thymus praecox arcticus* 'Coccineum'. Mother-of-thyme (8)

W *Convallaria majalis.* Lily-of-the-valley (12)

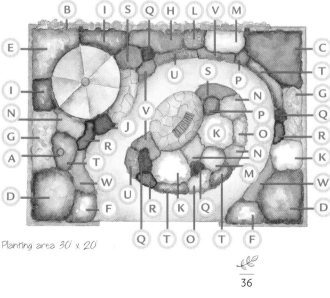

Planting area 30' x 20'

SOUTH AFRICAN MEDLEY A patio plan for mild climates (Zones 16, 17, 20–24) features plants from South Africa. Tall, drought-tolerant restios and leucadendrons form a privacy hedge around the patio, where five large, square glazed pots hold succulents, flowers, and a scented geranium. The sixth pot is fitted out with a solar-powered fountain. A collection of Mediterranean herbs fills a rectangular redwood planter near the sliding glass door, and a small table and chairs make an inviting spot in the corner.

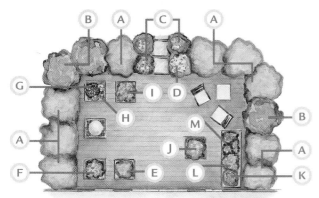

Deck area 26' x 16'

plant list

A *Ischyrolepis subverticillata.* Broom restio (9)

B *Leucadendron* 'Safari Sunshine' (3)

C *Osteospermum fruticosum* 'African Queen'. African daisy (3)

D *Arctotis acaulis.* African daisy (1)

E *Pelargonium tomentosum.* Peppermint geranium (1)

F *Felicia amelloides.* Blue marguerite (1)

G *Aeonium arboreum* 'Zwartkop' (1)

H *Echeveria* × *imbricata.* Hen and chicks (3)

I *Cotyledon orbiculata* (1)

J *Aloe striata.* Coral aloe (1)

K *Rosmarinus officinalis* 'Blue Spires'. Rosemary (1)

L *Salvia officinalis* 'Purpurascens'. Common sage (1)

M *Thymus vulgaris* 'Argenteus'. Silver thyme (3)

southwestern scene

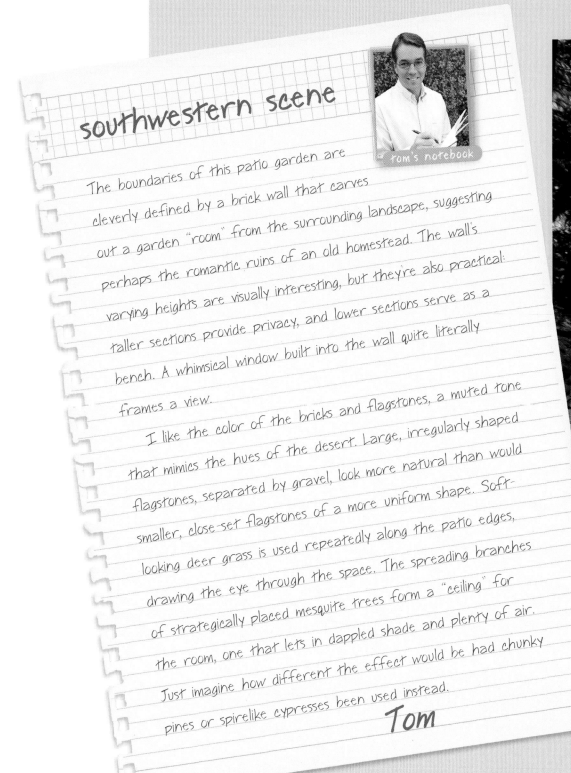

tom's notebook

The boundaries of this patio garden are cleverly defined by a brick wall that carves out a garden "room" from the surrounding landscape, suggesting perhaps the romantic ruins of an old homestead. The wall's varying heights are visually interesting, but they're also practical: taller sections provide privacy, and lower sections serve as a bench. A whimsical window built into the wall quite literally frames a view.

I like the color of the bricks and flagstones, a muted tone that mimics the hues of the desert. Large, irregularly shaped flagstones, separated by gravel, look more natural than would smaller, close-set flagstones of a more uniform shape. Soft-looking deer grass is used repeatedly along the patio edges, drawing the eye through the space. The spreading branches of strategically placed mesquite trees form a "ceiling" for the room, one that lets in dappled shade and plenty of air. Just imagine how different the effect would be had chunky pines or spirelike cypresses been used instead.

Tom

1 Sculptural cactus adds visual weight

2 Smooth stones suggest a small stream

3 Bright blue paint draws attention to the focal point

4 Low shrubs don't block the distant view

5 Lightweight furniture is easily moved and visually unobtrusive

plant list

A *Chamaerops humilis.*
Mediterranean fan palm (3)

B *Westringia fruticosa*
'Wynyabbie Gem'.
Coast rosemary (2)

C *Leptospermum scoparium*
'Snow White'.
New Zealand tea tree (2)

D *Phormium* 'Surfer'. (1)

E *Phormium tenax* 'Tom Thumb'.
New Zealand flax (1)

F *Vinca minor.*
Dwarf periwinkle (2)

G *Viola × wittrockiana.* Pansy (1)

H *Haworthia fasciata* (1)

I *Crassula falcata* (1)

SEACOAST BALCONY A dramatic view calls for plants with some stage presence. On this balcony, the addition of succulents, fan palms, and coast rosemary have transformed a stark space into a comfortable and inviting aerie, ideal for Zones 15–17, 20-24. The plants were chosen for year-round interest and for their adaptability to containers and to the seaside conditions. The casual arrangement of pots invites the gardener to reposition the plants throughout the growing season. As a final touch, a bistro table and chairs nestled among the plants give this narrow balcony the illusion of depth.

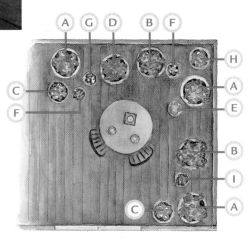

Deck area 8 x 8

A DECKSIDE RETREAT This cedar deck is made of 2 by 4s arranged in a pattern inspired by a Japanese fan, a shape that is repeated in the lawn area. Containers of herbs and perennials tie in the deck with the garden. The built-in seating area faces a modern stone fountain and river birch with salmon-colored bark that darkens to orange-brown and eventually peels off in sheets. This garden will do well in colder areas of the country, especially Zones 3–6 and 32–41.

plant list

A *Anemone blanda* 'White Splendor'. Greek windflower (10+)

B *Asarum europaeum.* European wild ginger (7)

C *Betula nigra* 'Heritage'. River birch (4)

D *Clematis* 'Hagley Hybrid' (3)

E *Crocus speciosus* 'Alba', *C. vernus* 'Snow Storm' (20+)

F *Euonymus fortunei* 'Sarcoxie'. Winter creeper (4)

G *Gaultheria procumbens.* Wintergreen (4)

H *Heuchera micrantha* 'Palace Purple'. Coral bells (6)

I *Parthenocissus tricuspidata.* Boston ivy (2)

J *Trillium sessile.* Wake robin (as underplanting)

K *Viola sororia* 'Freckles'. Dooryard violet (as underplanting)

L Annuals: *Ipomoea batatas* 'Blackie'. Sweet potato vine (4); *Pelargonium* 'Contrast'. Geranium (3); *Tagetes tenuifolia* 'Lemon Gem'. Signet marigold (6); *Thymophylla tenuiloba.* Dahlberg Daisy (6)

M Bulbs: *Narcissus* 'Golden Cheerfulness'. Daffodil (10+); *N.* 'Thalia' (20+); *Tulipa tarda.* Tulip (10+)

N Herbs: *Melissa officinalis* "Aurea". Lemon balm (6); *Thymus vulgaris* 'Silver Posie'. Common thyme

O Lawn: Kentucky bluegrass mix

P Perennials: *Coreopsis verticillata* 'Moonbeam' (6); *Rudbeckia hirta* Becky Mix. Black-eyed Susan (6)

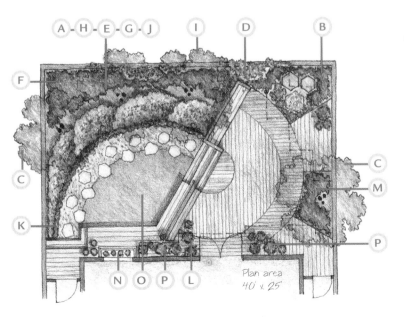

Plan area 40' x 25'

ALL DECKED OUT Ready for a long, warm summer, this deck brims with inviting color and enticing fragrances. Its anchor points are the two citrus trees that frame the trellises and provide a leafy, scented backdrop for the seating. In Zones 14–24, where these plants succeed (provided the angel's trumpet is protected from freezes in Zones 14 and 15), bloom begins in mid-spring and continues into fall. Long-flowering perennials are featured, and assorted annuals intensify the color.

plant list

A *Citrus* (lemon or orange) (2)
as underplanting: *Lobularia maritima*, white (sweet alyssum)

B *Brugmansia × candida.* Angel's trumpet (1)
as underplanting: *Gazania* hybrid, cream; *Helichrysum petiolare* 'Limelight' (licorice plant)

C *Abutilon megapotamicum.* Flowering maple (2, on trellises)
as underplanting: *Begonia* (bedding type, bronze leaves); *Liriope muscari* 'Silvery Sunproof' (big blue lily turf); *Campanula poscharskyana* (Serbian bellflower)

D *Buxus microphylla japonica.* Japanese boxwood (15)

E *Phormium* 'Maori Maiden' (1) as underplanting: *Petunia × hybrida*, pink; *Centaurea cineraria* (dusty miller); *Helichrysum petiolare* (licorice plant)

F *Heliotropium arborescens.* Common heliotrope (3)
as underplanting: *Brachyscome multifida* (Swan River daisy); *Verbena × hybrida*, white

G *Agapanthus* 'Peter Pan'. Lily-of-the-Nile (1)
as underplanting: *Nierembergia linariifolia* 'Mont Blanc' (dwarf cup flower); *Lobelia erinus* 'Crystal Palace'

H *Hemerocallis* 'Stella de Oro'. Daylily (2)
as underplanting: *Lobelia erinus*, white

I *Heuchera micrantha* 'Palace Purple'. Coral bells (4)

J *Echeveria × imbricata* (hen and chicks) (1); *Sedum sieboldii* (stonecrop) (1); *Sempervivum*, bronze cultivar (houseleek) (2)

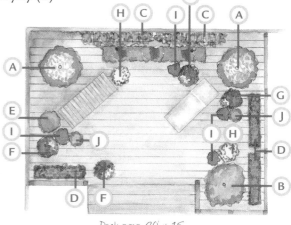

Deck area 20' x 15'

A SHADY RETREAT Cool and leafy, this deck is a serene oasis, a perfect place for just relaxing. Thanks to shade from house walls and off-deck trees, it's ideal for deckscaping with favorite shade plants. Unlike the sunny, mass-of-color plan shown opposite, this one gives you flower color in individual bursts off and on from winter through summer. But colorful and variegated foliage does offer a display throughout the growing season: coleus in a rainbow of hues, non-green foliage on hosta, dead nettle, bishop's weed, and heuchera. Try this plan in Zones 4–9, 14–21, being sure to move the potted fuchsia to a sheltered, frost-free spot during winter.

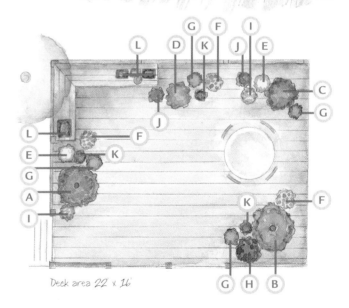

Deck area 22 x 16

plant list

A *Acer palmatum* 'Bloodgood'. Japanese maple (1)
   as underplanting: *Lamium maculatum* 'White Nancy' (dead nettle)

B *Camellia japonica* 'Nuccio's Pearl' (1)
   as underplanting: *Campanula poscharskyana* (Serbian bellflower)

C *Hydrangea macrophylla.* Bigleaf hydrangea (1)

D *Rhododendron (azalea)* 'Sherwood Pink' (1)

E *Aegopodium podagraria.* Bishop's weed (4)

F *Impatiens walleriana* (9)

G *Hosta* 'Gold Edger'. Plantain lily (4)

H *Fuchsia* 'Gartenmeister Bonstedt' (1)

I *Heuchera* 'Pewter Veil'. Coral bells (1)

J *Hosta sieboldiana* 'Elegans'. Plantain lily (2)

K *Solenostemon scutellarioides.* Coleus (6)

L All pots on slat bench are bonsai specimens

on the front porch | an old-fashioned charmer

A beautiful old house with a deep shady porch just begs to be filled with pots of plants and a seating area for sippping lemonade and watching the world go by. This porch filled with old-fashioned favorites such as geraniums, hydrangeas, and petunias plus lilies, daisies, and miniature roses captures that spirit perfectly.

plant list

A *Chrysanthemum frutescens.* Marguerite

B *Bracteantha bracteata.* Bush strawflower

C *Lilium.* Oriental lily

D *Hydrangea macrophylla.* Bigleaf hydrangea

E *Rosa,* miniature, pink and white

F *Caladium bicolor.* Fancy-leafed caladium

G *Asparagus densiflorus.*
Ornamental asparagus fern

H *Nephrolepis exaltata* 'Bostoniensis'.
Boston fern

I *Pelargonium,* pink and magenta varieties.
Geranium (3)

J *Petunia × hybrida,* white

K *Phalaenopsis* hybrid. Moth orchid

A wicker chair nestles between pots while cushions of flowers soften the porch's straight-edged design. Among the blooms are Oriental lilies, white 'Palace' miniature roses, white marguerites, yellow strawflowers, and pink hydrangeas.

A caladium and an ornamental asparagus fern form a billowy mound in the corner, while pink miniature roses punch up the foreground.

The destination may be the garden bench in the distance, but the path leading to it is equally enticing. Flagstones placed closely together provide a stable walking surface, but their irregular edges match the billowing softness of the surrounding plants. As an added bonus, pockets of plants within the path itself add visual interest along the way.

passageways

Paths and side yards are often overlooked when designing a landscape. The truth is, they're an essential part of any garden, so why not make them destinations in their own right?

A path can be more than just a strip that takes you from Point A to Point B. Choose material to match the surrounding garden—large pavers for a contemporary feel, flagstone stepping-stones that evoke a country theme, gravel to turn a landscape into a Mediterranean getaway. Then add plants to match, and you've created a garden element that can hold its own in a larger landscape.

Side yards are the neglected outdoor hallways, relegated to the status of a holding space for garbage cans and leftover lumber. They're often narrow strips, either dark and enclosed with high fences and walls or unbearably sunny thanks to minimal shading from surrounding plants or buildings. But clever design solutions, such as planters attached to a fence or a row of vine-covered trellises to create a shady path, can help these garden trouble spots. Even the narrowest space usually has room for a plant or two, and there are numerous solutions to the problems of sun and shade.

The ideas that follow will get you started. We also offer two ideas for that other often-neglected spot: the strip between the sidewalk and the street. It, too, can be more than just a landing pad for parked cars.

A stepping-stone path disappearing into the shrubbery adds an aura of mystery to even the smallest yard by giving the impression of another garden hidden just out of sight.

plant list

A *Eleutherococcus sieboldianus* 'Variegatus'.
Five-leaf aralia (1)

B *Viburnum × carlcephalum.* Fragrant snowball (2)

C *Acer japonicum* 'Aconitifolium'.
Fernleaf fullmoon maple (1)

D *Rhododendron (azalea)* 'Koromo Shikibu' (1)

E *Asarum europaeum.* Wild ginger (12)

F *Hosta* 'Francee'. Plantain lily (5)

G *Chamaecyparis pisifera* 'Snow'. Sawara false cypress (1)

H *Dryopteris erythrosora.* Autumn fern (5)

I *Euonymus alatus* 'Compacta'. Winged euonymus (1)

J *Buxus sempervirens* 'Elegantissima'.
Common boxwood (1)

K *Carex siderosticha* 'Variegata'. Sedge (5)

L *Hedera colchica.* Persian ivy (6)

SHADED PATHWAY Carefully spaced flagstones lead you through a garden border filled with shade-loving plants. The curving path hints at an unseen garden around the corner, while the brightly flowered azalea provides a splash of color that marks the start of the path. This garden was designed to do well in lightly shaded areas in Zones 8–9, 14–24, 29.

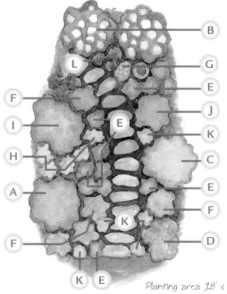

Planting area 18' x 28'

plant list

A *Amelanchier × grandiflora.* Serviceberry (1)

B *Clematis* 'Hagley Hybrid' (1)

C *Alchemilla mollis.* Lady's-mantle (4)

D *Polygonatum odoratum* 'Variegatum'. Solomon's seal (6)

E *Astrantia major.* Masterwort (3)

F *Astilbe × arendsii* 'Peach Blossom'. False spirea (4+)

G *Astilbe simplicifolia* 'Sprite'. False spirea (6)

H *Athyrium nipponicum* 'Pictum'. Japanese painted fern (5)

I *Brunnera macrophylla* 'Variegata'. Brunnera (4)

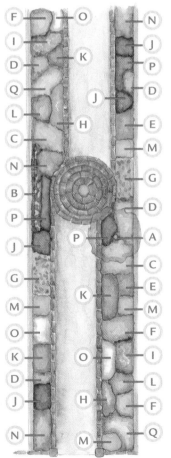

J *Heuchera* 'Pewter Veil'. Coral bells (4)

K *Corydalis flexuosa* 'Blue Panda' (6)

L *Hosta* 'Frances Williams'. Plantain lily (2)

M *Hosta* 'Shade Fanfare'. Plantain lily (4)

N *Hosta* 'Hadspen Blue'. Plantain lily (9+)

O *Pulmonaria saccharata* 'Mrs. Moon'. Bethlehem sage (6+)

P *Campanula portenschlagiana.* Dalmatian bellflower (6)

Q *Hakonechloa macra* 'Aureola'. Japanese forest grass (4)

Planting area 8' x 35'

PASSAGEWAY GARDEN Even a formal, essentially straight path offers an opportunity to transform a forgotten side yard into a passageway garden, with plantings that give you a reason to slow down and admire the view. The lively assortment shown here thrives in day-long dappled sun or light shade, or in a situation where sunny mornings are followed by light shade in the afternoon. Summer bloom time brings the brightest display, but you'll also enjoy more subtle color throughout the growing season. This plan does best in Zones 3–6, 32–35, 37, 39–41.

A WALK AMONG THE GRASSES Grasses look right at home lining a pathway. They soften hard edges and unify the space, providing interest throughout the growing season. In addition, many ornamental grasses have flowers that can add color and texture. In the garden here, designed for Zones 2–10, 14–27, 21–24, 29–41, the path to the gate gives you the feeling of walking through a tall-grass prairie.

plant list

A *Alopecurus pratensis* 'Aureus'. Yellow foxtail grass (6)

B *Calamagrostis × acutiflora* 'Karl Foerster'. Feather reed grass (3)

C *Echinacea purpurea* 'White Swan'. Coneflower (8)

D *Helenium* 'Moerheim Beauty'. Sneezeweed (3)

E *Helictotrichon sempervirens* 'Sapphire'. Blue oat grass (7)

F *Miscanthus sinensis* 'Silberfeder'. Eulalia, Japanese silver grass (1)

G *Schizachyrium scoparium* 'The Blues'. Little bluestem (3)

Planting area 18 x 9

plant list

A *Hemerocallis* 'Stella de Oro'. Daylily (5)

B *Berberis × thunbergii* 'Aurea'. Japanese barberry (1)

C *Phygelius rectus* 'Moonraker'. Cape fuchsia (1)

D *Nassella tenuissima.* Mexican feather grass (1)

E *Euphorbia characias wulfenii* (5)

F *Verbena bonariensis* (3)

G *Helictotrichon sempervirens.* Blue oat grass (2)

H *Knautia macedonica* (2)

I *Iris,* Siberian (3)

J *Coreopsis verticillata* 'Moonbeam' (2)

K *Phlomis fruticosa.* Jerusalem sage (1)

L *Alchemilla mollis.* Lady's-mantle (14)

M *Geranium nodosum.* Cranesbill (1)

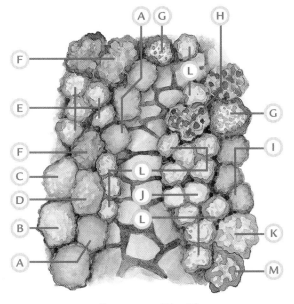

Planting area 20' x 24'

SPLENDOR IN THE GRASS Water-wise gardens may have a reputation for being sparse and plain, but this garden, which was designed for Zones 4–9, 14–24, demonstrates that unthirsty border plants can be extraordinarily beautiful. The ornamental grasses give beds a sense of constant motion, while daylilies soften pathway edges and dark-leafed trees provide the perfect backdrop to the array of textures and forms. The many shades of green are set off by gold, maroon, and magenta.

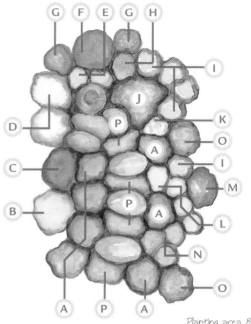

Planting area 8 x 10'

A BUTTERFLY BUFFET Provide food, and guests are guaranteed. It's true for people, and it's true for butterflies. This butterfly garden is filled with nectar-rich flowering plants that attract monarchs, swallowtails, and other winged visitors. There are also larval plants for their caterpillar offspring to chomp on, an urn fountain to sip from, and a trio of flat rocks for basking in the sun. For human visitors, the cushion-shaped concrete pads are equally inviting. Since the plants are perennials in Zones 8–9, 14–21, this garden is also easy to care for.

plant list

A *Lantana montevidensis.* Trailing lantana (7)

B *Aster cordifolius* 'Cape Cod'. Blue wood aster (1)

C *Aster cordifolius* 'Little Carlow'. Blue wood aster (1)

D *Aster* × *frikartii* 'Mönch' (2)

E *Achillea* 'Moonshine'. Yarrow (2)

F *Buddleja davidii nanhoensis.* Dwarf butterfly bush (1)

G *Penstemon* 'Midnight'. Border penstemon (2)

H *Penstemon* 'Sour Grapes'. Border penstemon (1)

I *Rudbeckia hirta* 'Indian Summer'. Gloriosa daisy (5)

J *Pittosporum tobira* 'Wheeler's Dwarf'. Tobira (1)

K *Echinacea purpurea* 'White Swan'. Coneflower (1)

L *Asclepias curassavica* 'Silky Gold'. Blood flower (4)

M *Gaura lindheimeri* (1)

N *Asclepias tuberosa.* Butterfly weed (3)

O *Carex buchananii.* Leather leaf sedge (2)

P *Thymus praecox arcticus.* Mother-of-thyme (4)

plant list

A *Lonicera × heckrottii*. Goldflame honeysuckle (4)

B *Ribes sanguineum*. Pink winter currant (1)

C *Digitalis × mertonensis*. Foxglove (7)

D *Iris foetidissima*. Gladwin iris (3)

E *Liriope muscari* 'Silvery Sunproof'. Big blue lily turf (6)

F *Polystichum polyblepharum*. Japanese tassel fern (2)

G *Bergenia cordifolia*. Heartleaf bergenia (5)

H × *Heucherella alba* 'Bridget Bloom' (6)

I *Corydalis lutea* (6)

J *Lamium maculatum* 'White Nancy'. Dead nettle (8)

K *Campanula poscharskyana*. Serbian bellflower (7+)

L *Ajuga reptans*. Carpet bugle (8)

M *Sagina subulata* 'Aurea'. Scotch moss (about twenty-two 3-inch squares, set 6 inches apart)

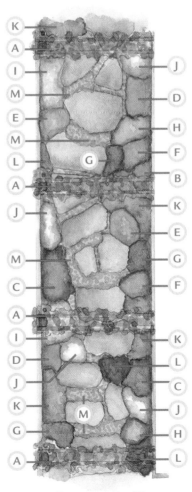

Planting area 8 × 30

DOWN THE GARDEN PATH In this side yard, a stone path leads through an inviting bower. Fragrant honeysuckle on the overheads gives a sense of enclosure, while various low-growing plants and ground covers provide a patchwork carpet of leaf and flower color, punctuated by vertical accents of foxglove and gladwin iris. Zones 4–9, 14–24, and 32 are congenial climates for this plan; color reaches its peak in spring.

natural connections

tom's notebook

Even if your side yard is not much wider than a wheelbarrow with a wide load, there's often just enough room for a garden. In this space, what was once a utilitarian path has been turned into a lush walkway that is a destination in its own right.

The oversized leaves and exotic, hanging flowers of angel's trumpet and flowering maple set a tropical tone. Siting the angel's trumpet near the kitchen window affords some privacy, and allows the sweet scent of its blooms to waft directly into the house. Stepping-stones of Mariposa slate are used to create an informal path that echoes the colors of the house trim and fence.

Concealed among evergreen ferns on either side of the path are wire baskets that hold pots of orchids from the owner's collection. In summer, when the orchids are in bloom, they're moved from the greenhouse into the garden, an idea that would work equally well with houseplants.

Tom

1

1 Colorful coleus are replaced with cyclamen in winter

2 A pot of white begonias on a stand brightens the darkest area

3 Ferns scattered throughout softly tie together the design

4 Hanging baskets of begonias make use of the vertical space

plant list

A *Agapanthus praecox orientalis.*
Lily-of-the-Nile (4)

B *Phormium* 'Yellow Wave' (1)

C *Hemerocallis,* cream cultivar.
Daylily (4)

D *Pennisetum setaceum* 'Burgundy
Blaze' ('Rubrum Dwarf').
Fountain grass (3)

E *Erigeron karvinskianus.*
Santa Barbara daisy (2)

F *Convolvulus cneorum.*
Bush morning glory (2)

G *Aloe maculata.* Soap aloe (4)

H *Echeveria × imbricata.*
Hen and chicks (5)

I *Osteospermum fruticosum.*
Trailing African daisy (6)

J *Oenothera speciosa.* Mexican evening
primrose (5)

K *Verbena* 'Tapien Purple'. Moss verbena (8)

L *Teucrium cossonii majoricum.* Germander (4)

M *Cerastium tomentosum.* Snow-in-summer (11)

Planting area 30 x 5.5

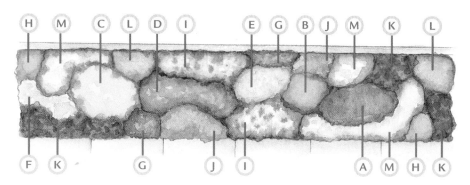

ROADSIDE RIOT Parking strips
offer a great gardening opportunity.
Despite their narrowness (widths
vary from 3 to about 6 feet), the
plots can pack in a dazzling variety
of colorful plants, affording both
you and passersby great pleasure.
You need tough plants and, often, a
rudimentary watering system: sand-
wiched between strips of pavement,
these areas can dry out rapidly.
In this planting (ideal for Zones
14–24), a kaleidoscope of California
favorites sizzles with color from
spring through summer.

plant list

A *Caryopteris × clandonensis.*
Blue mist (2)

B *Asclepias tuberosa.* Butterfly weed (1)

C *Liatris spicata* 'Kobold'.
Gayfeather (4)

D *Sedum* 'Autumn Joy'. Stonecrop (2)

E *Festuca glauca* 'Elijah Blue'.
Common blue fescue (9)

F *Gaillardia × grandiflora* 'Goblin'.
Blanket flower (10)

G *Hemerocallis* 'Stella de Oro'.
Daylily (7)

H *Achillea tomentosa.*
Woolly yarrow (10)

I *Salvia × sylvestris* 'May Night'.
Sage (14)

J *Iberis sempervirens* 'Snowflake'.
Evergreen candytuft (5)

K *Stachys byzantina* 'Silver Carpet'.
Lamb's ears (7)

TRAFFIC STOPPER Knockout color guaranteed! Blazing in hot hues (with a tempering touch of cool blue and purple), these plants are rugged customers, well suited to life on the street. They're impressively tolerant of varied climates too, thriving in Zones 3–9, 14–17, and 29–41, areas that encompass virtually the entire spectrum of summer and winter conditions. From late spring until autumn, you can count on an arresting show of colorful flowers. Aside from the shrubby blue mist, all the plants are perennials that need just an annual cleanup (in late fall or early spring, depending on climate) to stay tidy.

Planting area 30' x 5.5'

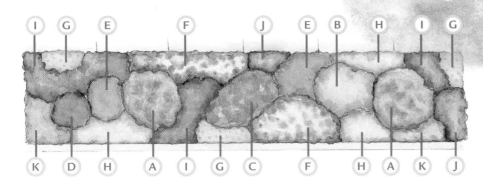

side yard surprise | creating a garden destination

Side yards are often treated as pass-throughs between the front and backyards, but in this garden, the two side yards were transformed into exciting destinations. A meandering 30-inch-wide path curves through the space, next to beds packed with blooming plants, including daylilies, lamb's ears, penstemon, society garlic, and hot pink verbena. A spacious patio is the ideal spot to view the entire garden, while, at back, a crape myrtle marks the transition to the backyard. The plants in these beds were layered from shortest in front to tallest in back, letting each plant shine. Many were gifts from friends, and bloomers like alyssum and lobelia are allowed to reseed freely. To avoid making a small space look messy, the designer has stuck to a color scheme of purple, pink, yellow, and a little white.

A low bench is nearly hidden in the lush border. To keep the garden from being overgrown, about an hour per week is spent deadheading, weeding, and cutting back any plants that have grown out of bounds.

The large dining patio, perfect for family meals and entertaining, is accessible from indoors via the step at right, allowing for easy movement from the house to the garden.

plant list

A *Hemerocallis* hybrids. Daylilies

B *Stachys byzantina.* Lamb's ears

C *Penstemon* hybrids. Border penstemon

D *Tulbaghia violacea.* Society garlic

E *Verbena × hybrida.* Garden verbena

F *Alstroemeria* hybrids

G *Lobelia erinus*

H *Chrysanthemum maximum.* Shasta daisy

I *Lobularia maritima.* Sweet alyssum

J *Salvia leucantha.* Mexican bush sage

K *Lavatera thuringiaca* 'Barnsley'. Tree mallow

L *Lagerstroemia* hybrid. Crape myrtle

M *Cuphea hyssopifolia.* False heather

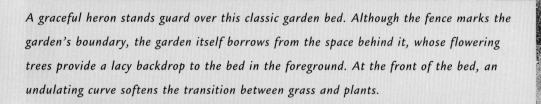

A graceful heron stands guard over this classic garden bed. Although the fence marks the garden's boundary, the garden itself borrows from the space behind it, whose flowering trees provide a lacy backdrop to the bed in the foreground. At the front of the bed, an undulating curve softens the transition between grass and plants.

beds and borders

When most people hear the word "garden," beds and borders are what comes to mind. They are garden mainstays that link the garden "floor," the grass or ground cover, to the garden "ceiling," the sky. They can create a backdrop, mark a garden edge, or delineate garden "rooms" and special-use areas.

Beds and borders give gardeners the opportunity to shape their overall space into the look they want and fill it with plants they love. The result can be plain or elaborate, country casual or modern sophisticate, tiny pockets of space or expansive sweeps of repeated plantings.

These spaces are the most versatile areas of any garden design. They can be created with in-ground plantings, in raised beds, even by using pots. They can be composed of the same or similar plants, or feature a mixture of shrubs, trees, annuals, and perennials with some grasses thrown in for good measure. The colors can range from a serene monochromatic blend to a crazy-quilt scheme designed to enliven a space.

The following 25 plans offer a wealth of ideas for beds and borders. Look for one that works for you—or experiment with a mix of ideas. The end result will be a garden that reflects your personal style.

These heat-loving succulents are the perfect choices for this Southwest garden. The strong colors contrast with the stark white of the garden wall.

blue heron
farm pump
asian inspired
jug
bird bath
pedestal

windmill
fence
stones
wall
fountain
waterfall

arbor
bench
pool
trellis

COLORFUL TAPESTRY Once a flat, blank space, this garden is now a multilayered planting bed filled with conifers, annuals, and bulbs. The pines and spruce anchor the planting and provide year-round foliage interest. Annuals and tender perennials add summer color, and hardy perennials are reliable repeat performers. This garden flourishes in Zone 2, but will also thrive in Zones 1–9, 14–17, 32–43 (dig and store bulbs in the coldest climates).

plant list

A *Spiraea nipponica* 'Snowmound'. Spirea (1)

B *Lonicera japonica*. Japanese honeysuckle (1)

C *Pinus flexilis* 'Vanderwolf's Pyramid'. Limber pine (1)

D *Scabiosa columbaria* 'Pink Mist'. Pincushion flower (2)

E *Salvia × sylvestris* 'May Night'. Sage (3)

F *Picea pungens* 'Glauca Globosa'. Dwarf globe Colorado blue spruce (1)

G *Iris*. Bearded iris (1)

H *Pinus sylvestris* 'Glauca Nana'. Dwarf blue Scotch pine (1)

I *Dianthus* 'First Love'. Pink (3)

J *Agapanthus praecox orientalis*. Lily-of-the-Nile (2)

K *Pinus mugo* 'Slowmound'. Mugho pine (1)

L *Petunia × hybrida,* red and white varieties (12)

M *Viola tricolor*. Johnny-jump-up (5)

N *Viola × wittrockiana* 'Jolly Joker'. Pansy (10)

O *Crocosmia* 'Lucifer' (2)

P *Alcea rosea*. Hollyhock (2)

Q *Leonotis leonurus*. Lion's tail (3)

R *Verbena bonariensis* (3)

S *Iris sibirica*. Siberian iris (1)

T *Rosa* 'Flower Carpet White' (1)

U *Hosta* 'So Sweet'. Plantain lily (2)

V *Ricinus communis*. Castor bean (2)

W *Pinus mugo uncinata*. Dwarf Swiss mountain pine (1)

X *Rhododendron albiflorum*. Cascade azalea (1)

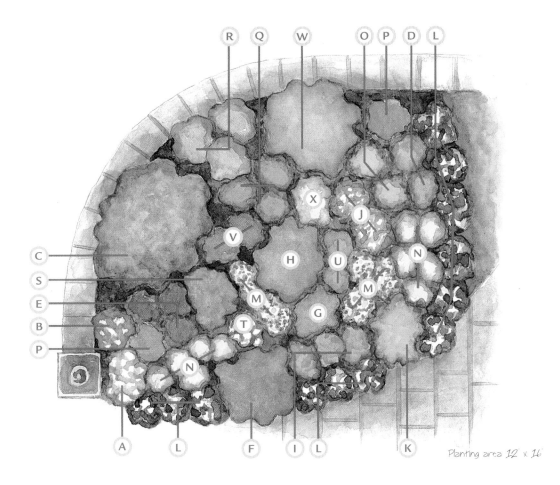

Planting area 12 × 16

Planting area 20' x 8'

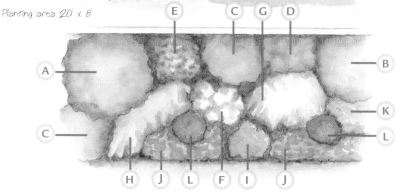

SHADED FENCE FOR THE SUNBELT

Over much of California's Zones 14–24 and throughout the Southeast's Zones 31 and 32, summers are warm to hot. In these areas, summer shade is a welcome relief for people but may not always suit plants. This assortment, though, is perfectly at home in very light shade all day, or with a little morning sun followed by light shade in the afternoon. There's no peak season for flower color; you can enjoy it in all seasons, from winter's camellia through fall's Japanese anemone and the last of the impatiens. Heuchera, lily turf, and Japanese forest grass provide subtle but steady foliage color throughout the growing season.

plant list

A *Camellia japonica* 'Nuccio's Pearl' (1)

B *Rhododendron (azalea)* 'George Lindley Taber' (1)

C *Rhododendron (azalea)* 'Hinodegiri' (2)

D *Anemone × hybrida.* Japanese anemone (3)

E *Digitalis × mertonensis.* Foxglove (4)

F *Helleborus argutifolius.* Corsican hellebore (2)

G *Hakonechloa macra* 'Aureola'. Japanese forest grass (3)

H *Liriope muscari* 'Variegata'. Big blue lily turf (5)

I *Heuchera micrantha.* 'Palace Purple'. Coral bells (2)

J *Ajuga reptans.* Carpet bugle (14+)

K *Campanula poscharskyana.* Serbian bellflower (3+)

L *Impatiens walleriana* (annuals, in pots)

SHADED FENCE FOR COLDER CLIMES Where houses are fairly close together, shade is sure to affect plantings along a fence or wall. Those areas will be dimmer and cooler (and for more hours of the day) where houses are tall and mature trees grow nearby. But you can still enjoy a visually interesting planting punctuated by floral color. The scheme shown here works well in Zones 3–6, 32–41, where plants will thrive in light to moderate shade all day if given regular watering. Summer is the most colorful season: bergenia and hosta foliage is at its most striking, and meadow rue, masterwort, astilbe, and summersweet are all abloom.

Planting area 20' x 8'

plant list

A *Clethra alnifolia.* Summersweet (1)

B *Rhododendron* 'PJM' (2)

C *Thalictrum rochebrunianum.* Meadow rue (6)

D *Astrantia major.* Masterwort (5+)

E *Polystichum acrostichoides.* Christmas fern (4)

F *Hosta sieboldiana* 'Elegans'. Plantain lily (2)

G *Astilbe simplicifolia* 'Sprite'. False spirea (5)

H *Bergenia* 'Bressingham Ruby' (2)

I × *Heucherella* 'Pink Frost' (4)

J *Convallaria majalis.* Lily-of-the-valley (8+)

HOT AND SPICY The colors of this front yard aren't for everyone; it takes courage to put on such a bold show. In early spring, bright orange flowers contrast beautifully with foliage in deep purple, dark green, and lime green—with tall red and yellow tulips as accents. "It's a busy garden," says the designer, "but the masses of orange make it work." This garden works in Zones 2–10, 12–14, 30–45, though the tulips will need to be treated as annuals in mild climates.

plant list

A *Papaver nudicaule.* Iceland poppy (3)

B *Tulipa* 'Yellow Emperor' (11)

C *Tulipa,* red lily-flowered variety (8)

D *Nemesia strumosa,* orange variety (5)

E *Tulipa* 'Corsage' (5)

F *Chrysanthemum parthenium* 'Aureum'. Feverfew (4)

G *Lilium* 'Fire King' or 'Avignon'. Lily (3)

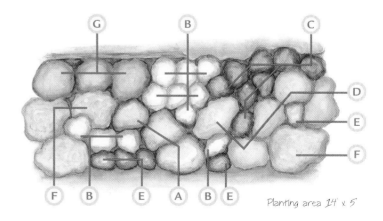

Planting area 14 x 5

BEAUTIFUL BOUNDARY Some fences are quite open in structure—as here, where a post-and-rail fence defines the edge of a cultivated garden while allowing a clear view into the wild meadow beyond. Given regular moisture and a full-sun location, this floral medley delivers a summer's worth of color. The plants are all herbaceous perennials, dying back to the ground or to low tufts of foliage when the growing season ends. A quick cleanup in late winter readies the planting for spring growth. This plan is especially well suited to Zones 32–41 but will also succeed in Zones 2–9, 14–21.

plant list

A *Hibiscus moscheutos* 'Blue River II'. Perennial hibiscus (1)

B *Echinacea purpurea* 'Magnus'. Purple coneflower (4+)

C *Liatris spicata* 'Kobold'. Gayfeather (2)

D *Geranium psilostemon* (2+)

E *Hemerocallis* 'Black-eyed Stella'. Daylily (2)

F *Coreopsis grandiflora* 'Early Sunrise' (4+)

G *Salvia* × *sylvestris* 'May Night'. Sage (7+)

H *Chrysanthemum maximum* 'Snow Lady'.
   Shasta daisy (3)

I *Nepeta* × *faassenii*. Catmint (6+)

J *Iberis sempervirens.* Evergreen candytuft (5)

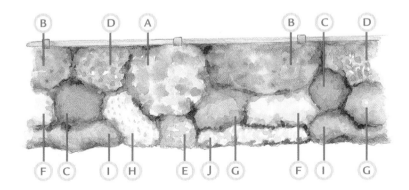

Planting area 22' × 6'

plant list

A *Echinacea purpurea.* Purple coneflower (1)

B *Cuphea hyssopifolia.* False heather (4)

C *Gaura lindheimeri* 'Passionate Blush' (2)

D *Salvia* 'Waverly'. Sage (2)

E *Heuchera micrantha* 'Palace Purple'. Coral bells (4)

F *Pennisetum setaceum* 'Rubrum'. Fountain grass (2)

G *Artemisia pycnocephala* 'David's Choice'. Sandhill sage (4)

H *Pennisetum setaceum* 'Eaton Canyon'. Fountain grass (1)

I *Abutilon* hybrid 'Mobile Pink'. Flowering maple (2)

J *Hydrangea macrophylla.* Bigleaf hydrangea (1)

COOL PERENNIALS A new twist on the pink theme, a border that pairs pink-flowered plants with subtle splashes of gray, green, and maroon foliage is more sophisticated than sweet. The border curves between the back fence and a deck to offer a picture-perfect view from the house. These plants do well in sun to part shade, especially in warmer climates, in Zones 14–24.

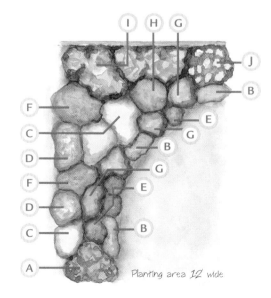

Planting area *12'* wide

plant list

A *Anisodontea × hypomandarum.* Cape mallow (1)

B *Erysimum* 'Bowles Mauve'. Wallflower (1)

C *Verbena bonariensis* (1)

D *Penstemon* 'Sour Grapes'. Border penstemon (3)

E *Agapanthus praecox orientalis* 'Albus'. Lily-of-the-Nile (1)

F *Erigeron karvinskianus.* Santa Barbara daisy (4+)

G *Helichrysum italicum.* Curry plant (2)

H *Aloe maculata.* Soap aloe (2)

I *Osteospermum fruticosum.* Trailing African daisy (4+)

J *Scaevola* 'Mauve Clusters' (2)

K *Convolvulus sabatius.* Ground morning glory (2)

L *Stachys byzantina* 'Silver Carpet'. Lamb's ears (5+)

FLORIFEROUS FENCEROW Set against a weathered wooden fence, this lush-looking planting needs only moderate water to provide good color from spring into fall. The scheme is intended for a sunny location in California's Zones 14–24, where winters are mild, summers are warm to hot, and water is at a premium. It's a relatively low-maintenance planting: one round of cleanup and discretionary pruning in winter will prepare it for a return engagement the next year.

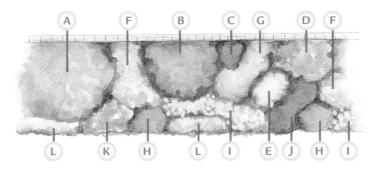

Planting area 22 × 6

plant list

A *Prunus × cistena.*
Dwarf red-leaf plum (1)

B *Paeonia suffruticosa.*
Tree peony (3)

C *Gypsophila paniculata.*
Baby's breath (2)

D *Hemerocallis,* yellow
cultivar. Daylily (8)

E *Geranium × magnificum* (4)

F *Geranium himalayense*
'Plenum' (3)

G *Heuchera micrantha* 'Palace
Purple'. Coral bells (3)

H *Sedum* 'Autumn Joy'.
Stonecrop (2)

I *Salvia × sylvestris*
'May Night'. Sage (10+)

J *Dianthus* 'Aqua'. Pink (8)

K *Potentilla nepalensis*
'Miss Willmott'.
Cinquefoil (8)

PICTURE PERFECT Plantings along a house soften the landscape, creating a transition from man-made structure to natural environment. Where foundation plantings are easily seen from a window, you'll want to create an especially eye-pleasing scheme. One such "picture window" design is shown here, offering colorful flowers and foliage from earliest spring into autumn. This mixture prefers regular moisture but will forgive occasional lapses. It may be satisfied by natural rainfall in Zones 32–39, but you'll surely need to provide some water in Zones 3–9, 14–16, 18–21. Substitute *Geranium* 'Ann Folkard' for *G. × magnificum* (E in the list at right) and the plan can also be enjoyed in Zones 2, 40, and 41.

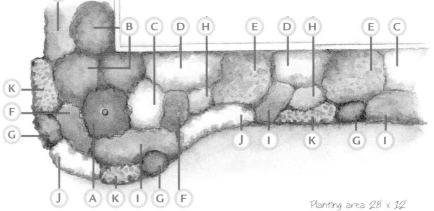

Planting area 28 × 12

WINDOW VIEW In regions where water is scant or expensive, the gardener's challenge is to create plantings with limited thirst. In California's Zones 8, 9, 14–24, rainfall may take care of winter water needs, but the warm months are typically too dry to support a varied garden without some assistance from the hose. The scheme shown here follows the same plot plan as "Picture Perfect" (facing page), but it uses plants that will prosper with less than regular watering. Flower color is present from spring into fall, but it crests in the summer display depicted below.

plant list

A *Buddleja davidii* 'Dark Knight'. Butterfly bush (1)

B *Phlomis fruticosa.* Jerusalem sage (3)

C *Lavandula × intermedia* 'Provence'. Lavandin (2)

D *Pennisetum setaceum* 'Rubrum'. Fountain grass (5)

E *Coleonema pulchellum* 'Sunset Gold'. Pink breath of heaven (2)

F *Achillea × taygetea.* Yarrow (5)

G *Convolvulus cneorum.* Bush morning glory (3)

H *Kniphofia uvaria* 'Little Maid'. Red-hot poker (2)

I *Erigeron karvinskianus.* Santa Barbara daisy (6+)

J *Verbena* 'Tapien Purple'. Moss verbena (7)

K *Gazania* 'Burgundy' (10)

Achillea

Heliotropium arborescens

plant list

A *Geranium* 'Pink Spice' (4)

B *Carex comans* 'Frosty Curls'.
New Zealand hair sedge (4)

C *Heliotropium arborescens*.
Common heliotrope (2)

D *Fuchsia magellanica* 'Versicolor' (1)

E *Pelargonium* 'Chocolate Mint'.
Scented geranium (2)

F *Sutera cordata* 'Golden Anniversary'.
Bacopa (3)

DEEP IN THE SHADE This border flies in the face of the common gardening philosophy that says shady areas should be filled with light-colored plants. Instead, a collection of dark and variegated foliage colors are highlighted with a splash of lime green to affect a cool, alluring setting. This garden will thrive in Zones 3–9, 14–24, 28–43 if the less hardy plants are treated as annuals. Frequent trimming is the key to keeping the border in-bounds and looking its best.

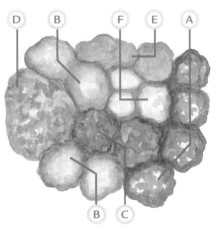

Planting area 8 x 6

SHADEMASTERS Shadows will be especially deep and cool in any nooks on the shady side of your house. Fortunately, this garden proves you needn't consign these darker regions to ivy and moss. The grouping illustrated below offers both subtle foliage color and periodic floral color. The birdbath rises from a "pool" of blue scaevola blossoms (or a real pond, if you prefer). With regular watering, this planting will thrive in all-day light shade in Zones 8, 9, 14–24. By substituting epimedium (*Epimedium* × *rubrum* 'Snow Queen') for vancouveria (J in the list below) and carpet bugle *(Ajuga reptans)* for scaevola (K), you can achieve virtually the same effect in Zones 4–7, 32, and 33.

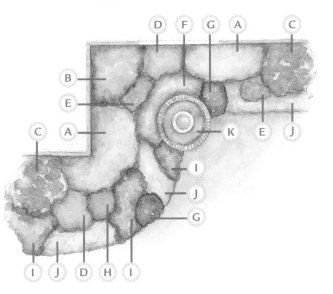

Plan 17' wide along window wall

plant list

A *Rhododendron (azalea)* 'Gumpo' (4)

B *Aucuba japonica.* Japanese aucuba (1)

C *Hydrangea macrophylla* 'Tricolor'. Bigleaf hydrangea (2)

D *Brunnera macrophylla.* Brunnera (2)

E *Adenophora confusa.* Lady bells (4)

F *Liriope muscari* 'Variegata'. Big blue lily turf (6)

G *Bergenia* 'Bressingham Ruby' (2)

H *Iris foetidissima.* Gladwin iris (1)

I × *Heucherella* 'Pink Frost' (7+)

J *Vancouveria hexandra* (7+)

K *Scaevola* 'Mauve Clusters' (3)

plant list

A *Scabiosa caucasica* 'Fama'. Pincushion flower (3)

B *Calendula officinalis*, Fiesta strain (1)

C *Viola* 'Cream Crown'. Pansy (4)

D *Narcissus* 'Mount Hood'. Daffodil
(grow for foliage) (1)

E *Viola × wittrockiana* 'Maxim'. Pansy (3)

F *Nepeta × faassenii* 'Blue Wonder'. Catmint (1)

G *Iberis sempervirens*. Evergreen candytuft (2)

H *Sedum* 'Autumn Joy'. Stonecrop (1)

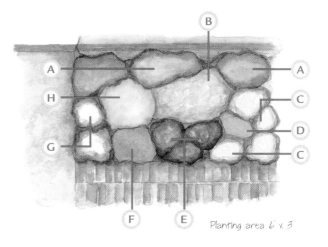

Planting area 6' × 3'

A GLINT OF SUNSHINE Annuals can be the mainstay of a winter garden. This pocket garden, designed to enliven a tiny corner, is filled with cool, soft purples and lemon yellows, and is nearly everblooming in Zone 15. Blend the plants within a small to medium garden bed, and the end result will be a garden that is colorful, yet peaceful. Even if your winters are too cold for winter color, these annuals can still provide a sunny lift to the garden in all zones in warmer seasons.

plant list

A *Lagerstroemia* 'Zuni'.
Crape myrtle (1)

B *Teucrium fruticans*.
Bush germander (3)

C *Nerium oleander* 'Petite Salmon'.
Oleander (3)

D *Punica granatum* 'Nana'.
Dwarf pomegranate (3)

E *Tecoma capensis* 'Aurea'.
Cape honeysuckle (1)

F *Pittosporum tobira* 'Wheeler's
Dwarf'. Tobira (3+)

G *Dietes iridioides*. Fortnight lily (2)

H *Erigeron karvinskianus*.
Santa Barbara daisy (5)

I *Santolina chamaecyparissus*.
Lavender cotton (2)

J *Achillea × taygetea*. Yarrow (3)

K *Teucrium × lucidrys*
'Prostratum'. Germander (8)

L *Oenothera speciosa*.
Mexican evening primrose (3)

HOT SPOTS Spend a bit of time near a sunny south-facing house wall, and soon you're gasping for breath. But while the environment may be too hot for most people, a variety of good-looking plants thrive in just these spots. This gathering features natives of regions where blistering summers are the norm; given the same conditions in your garden, they'll feel right at home. (Flowering is at its peak in summer, too.) Try this plan in desert Zones 12 and 13, as well as in Zones 14, 18–21.

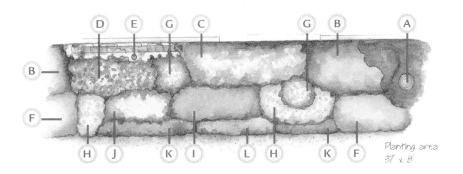

Planting area
37' x 8'

bold backdrop | standout border frames a pool

Inspired by the bold foliage and vibrant colors of tropical gardens, this border may have been designed as a backdrop, but it can hold its own in any landscape. The vegetation spills from a two-tiered planting bed designed as a setting for the pool and as a living screen concealing the fence at the back of the property. To the left, a bed of perennial cranesbill will soon spill over the stone wall, further blurring the pool's edges.

Stone stairs lead past the magnolia and to a second sitting terrace tucked away behind a thick hedge of heavenly bamboo.

The brilliantly colored plants spilling into the water at the pool's end all but obsure the flow from a spouting fountain.

plant list

A *Ipomoea batatas* 'Marguerite' Sweet potato vine

B *Tradescantia pallida* 'Purpurea'. Purple queen

C *Dahlia* 'Bishop of Landaff'

D *Colocasia esculenta* 'Black Magic'. Taro, elephant's ear

E *Solenostemon scutellarioides.* Coleus

F *Geranium macrorrhizum.* Cranesbill

G *Magnolia*

H *Nandina domestica.* Heavenly bamboo

PLENTY OF PERENNIALS This colorful group of easygoing late-spring and summer bloomers offers treats for all comers, including birds, butterflies, and human visitors. Most of these plants do well in almost all zones, although if you live in a very cold-winter climate, you will need to treat some tender perennials as annuals. The rest can remain in place for many years, requiring only a yearly late-winter cleanup.

A PERENNIAL SOLO A border composed entirely of perennials provides a spectacular display. This border contains five different perennials and a total of 13 plants. All are easy to grow, with blooms that will last for many weeks. These plants do well in Zones 2–10, 14–24, 30, 32–33, 37, 39.

plant list

A *Agastache rugosa.* Korean hummingbird mint (1)

B *Alcea rosea.* Hollyhock (6)

C *Centranthus ruber* 'Albus'. Jupiter's beard (1)

D *Asclepias tuberosa.* Butterfly weed (3)

E *Achillea filipendulina* 'Coronation Gold'. Fernleaf yarrow (2)

F *Achillea millefolium.* Common yarrow (4)

G *Echinacea purpurea.* Purple coneflower (3)

H *Chrysanthemum maximum* 'Alaska'. Shasta daisy (7)

I *Coreopsis grandiflora* 'Early Sunrise' or 'Sunburst' (12)

J *Liatris spicata.* Gayfeather (1)

K *Sedum* 'Autumn Joy'. Stonecrop (3)

L *Salvia nemorosa* 'Ostfriesland'. Sage (3)

M *Heuchera sanguinea.* Coral bells (9)

N *Cleome hasslerana.* Spider flower (1)

O *Dianthus gratianopolitanus.* Cheddar pink (4)

P *Iberis sempervirens* 'Snowflake'. Evergreen candytuft (4)

Q *Antirrhinum majus,* Rocket strain. Snapdragon (6)

R *Tagetes erecta.* African marigold (4)

S *Tagetes patula.* French marigold (6)

T *Nicotiana alata,* Nicki strain. Flowering tobacco (10)

U *Salvia splendens.* Scarlet sage (4)

V *Cosmos bipinnatus,* Sonata series (4)

W *Petunia* × *hybrida* (5)

X *Lobularia maritima.* Sweet alyssum (8)

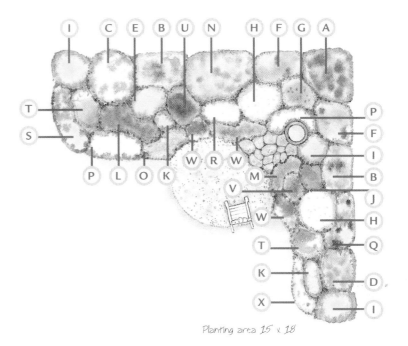

Planting area 15' x 18'

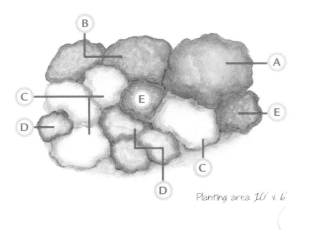

Planting area 10' x 6'

plant list

A *Perovskia.* Russian sage (1)

B *Echinacea purpurea.* Purple coneflower (2)

C *Coreopsis verticillata* 'Moonbeam' (4)

D *Nepeta* × *faassenii.* Catmint (4)

E *Scabiosa caucasica.* Pincushion flower (2)

plant list

A *Bergenia cordifolia* 'Perfect'. Heartleaf bergenia (3)

B *Alchemilla mollis.* Lady's-mantle (3)

C *Salvia nemorosa.* Sage (2)

D *Geranium* 'Anne Thompson'. Cranesbill (1)

E *Lysimachia punctata* 'Alexander'. Loosestrife (2)

F *Miscanthus sinensis* 'Pünktchen'. Eulalia, Japanese silver grass (3)

G *Kniphofia uvaria* 'Primrose Beauty'. Red-hot poker (2)

H *Dahlia* 'Bednail Beauty' (1)

HOT AND COLD This border went through several rounds of mixing and matching, but the final result is magnificent. Bergenias and lady's-mantle set the tone with contrasting shades of green, the Japanese silver grass forms a soft background, and red-hot poker packs a punch of color. Grow this mix of plants in Zones 2–9, 14–24, 31–43.

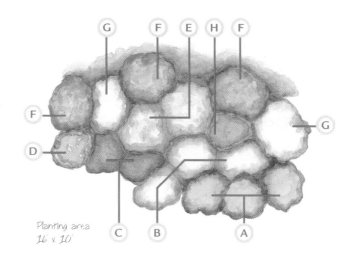

Planting area
16' x 10'

Planting area 28' x 12'

plant list

A *Amsonia hubrichtii.* Hubricht's bluestar (2)

B *Eryngium amethystinum.* Sea holly (4)

C *Euonymus alatus* 'Rudy Haag'. Winged euonymus (1)

D *Genista tinctoria* 'Royal Gold'. Dyer's greenweed (2)

E *Geranium macrorrhizum* 'Ingwersen's Variety'. Cranesbill (5)

F *Juniperus chinensis sargentii* 'Glauca'. Sargent juniper (1)

G *Lonicera sempervirens.* Trumpet honeysuckle (1)

H *Physocarpus opulifolius* 'Dart's Gold'. Common ninebark (1)

I *Rhus aromatica* 'Gro-Low'. Fragrant sumac (2)

J *Rosa* 'New Dawn' (1)

K *Scabiosa columbaria* 'Butterfly Blue'. Pincushion flower (5)

L *Solidago* 'Golden Baby'. Goldenrod (5)

M *Spiraea japonica* 'Goldmound'. Spirea (2)

N *Thuja occidentalis* 'Emerald'. American arborvitae (1)

O *Thymus praecox arcticus.* Mother-of-thyme (many)

P *Viburnum dentatum* 'Autumn Jazz'. Arrowwood (11)

A VISUAL FEAST Shrubs don't have to remain in the background while the perennials and annuals shine. This shrubby border's blooms and foliage give it color from spring through fall. And in winter, the dark green juniper and emerald green arborvitae take center stage. The border is surprisingly hardy as well, growing in Zones 2–10, 14–21, 32–43 (replace Hubricht's bluestar [A] with another choice in Zones 34–43).

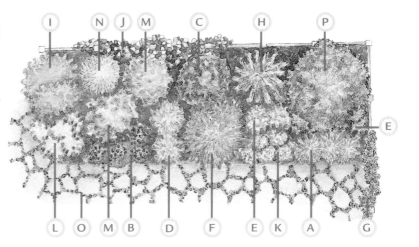

Leonotis leonurus

Salvia uliginosa

plant list

A *Salvia uliginosa.* Bog sage (2)

B *Nepeta × faassenii.* Catmint (3)

C *Lavandula × intermedia.* Lavandin (1)

D *Leonotis leonurus.* Lion's tail (1)

E *Olea europaea* 'Little Ollie'. Olive (1)

F *Penstemon* 'Midnight'.
Border penstemon (1)

G *Erigeron karvinskianus.*
Santa Barbara daisy (1)

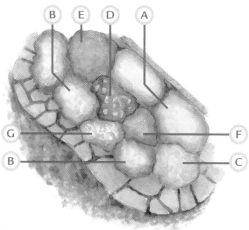

Planting area 11' x 5'

SUNNY BORDER Flowers that bloom over a long season and require only modest amounts of water or time—isn't that what we all want? This flower border gives you just that. It's made up entirely of plants adapted to a Mediterranean climate in shades of blue with touches of dark orange and patches of white to complement the scheme. Grow this garden in Zones 8-9, 14-24, H1, H2.

SIZZLING FALL BORDER Designing a late-season flower border requires balancing an eye-catching display that looks good in fall without sacrificing spring bloom. This border with long-blooming ground covers, perennials, and shrubs is a perfect solution to carry the show through the seasons. The garden is designed for Zones 4–9, 14–24.

Planting area 15´ x 8´

plant list

A *Verbena* 'Babylon Purple' (2)

B *Zinnia* 'Profusion Orange' (2)

C *Carex flagellifera* 'Toffee Twist'. Sedge (3)

D *Pennisetum setaceum* 'Rubrum'. Fountain grass (3)

E *Rosa* 'Mandarin Sunblaze' (2)

F *Perovskia* 'Blue Spire'. Russian sage (3)

G *Leonotis leonurus.* Lion's tail (3)

H *Buddleja davidii* 'Black Knight'. Butterfly bush (1)

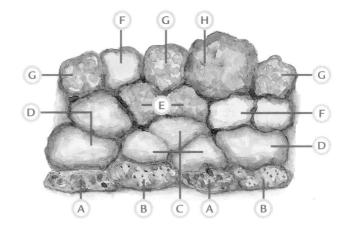

Hosta

plant list

A *Clematis,* herbaceous (1)

B *Paeonia,* herbaceous. Peony (1)

C *Euphorbia amygdaloides robbiae.*
Mrs. Robb's bonnet (2)

D *Hosta fortunei aureomarginata.*
Plantain lily (1)

E *Artemisia vulgaris* 'Oriental Limelight' (1)

F *Hakonechloa macra* 'Aureola'.
Japanese forest grass (1)

G *Acer palmatum* 'Crimson Queen'.
Japanese maple (1)

H *Chamaecyparis obtusa* 'Fernspray Gold'.
Hinoki false cypress (1)

I *Brunnera macrophylla* 'Hadspen Cream'.
Brunnera (1)

GREENS TO ENVY For impact, keep the color scheme basic. The various leaf textures and shapes of the plants play off one another, but by limiting the color palette to just two hues—lime green and red—the garden still looks cohesive. These plantings do best in Zones 2–9, 14–20, 31–34, but you can tailor this garden to any climate zone.

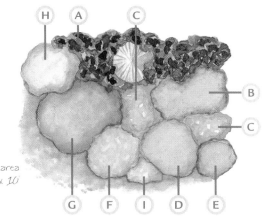

Planting area
14' x 10'

GRASSY BLEND The decorative grasses in this plan come in all shapes, sizes, and colors: foliage in fountains, shafts, and tussocks; blossoms and seed heads in spikes and plumes; colors ranging from steely blue-gray to rusty red. Many change still more in autumn. Mixing in bright flowers and a dramatic annual highlights the grasses even further. This garden will do well in Zones 2–10, 14–24.

plant list

A *Miscanthus sinensis* 'Strictus'. Porcupine grass (2)

B *Calamagrostis × acutiflora* 'Karl Foerster'. Feather reed grass (1)

C *Panicum virgatum* 'Haense Herms'. Switch grass (2)

D *Pennisetum orientale*. Oriental fountain grass (2)

E *Miscanthus sinensis* 'Yaku Jima'. Eulalia, Japanese silver grass (1)

F *Helictotrichon sempervirens*. Blue oat grass (1)

G *Pennisetum alopecuroides* 'Hameln'. Fountain grass (1)

H *Imperata cylindrica* 'Rubra'. Japanese blood grass (3)

I *Deschampsia cespitosa*. Tufted hair grass (2)

J *Festuca glauca* 'Elijah Blue'. Common blue fescue (5)

K *Rhynchelytrum nerviglume* 'Pink Crystals'. Natal ruby grass (2)

L *Rudbeckia fulgida* (3)

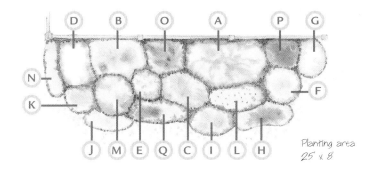

Planting area
25 × 8

M *Phlomis russeliana* (2)

N *Hemerocallis* 'Stella de Oro'. Daylily (4)

O *Tithonia rotundifolia*. Mexican sunflower (1)

P *Ricinus communis* 'Dwarf Red Spire'. Castor bean (1)

Q *Celosia*, Castle series. Plume cockscomb (7)

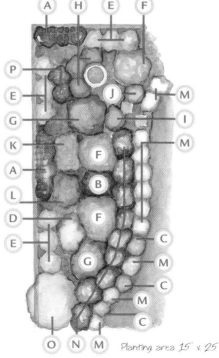

EASY-CARE COLOR Soft curves, layered plantings, year-round good looks, and a color palette of vivid pink and soft purple are the mainstays of this garden border. Designed also for ease of maintenance, it succeeds on all counts. In winter, evergreens become the main attraction and give form to the bed. But there are still some surprises: in early spring, dahlias and gladiolus pop into view. Plant this garden in Zones 13–17, 21–24.

plant list

A *Bougainvillea* 'Barbara Karst' (2)

B *Phormium* 'Sundowner' (1)

C *Tulbaghia violacea* 'Silver Lace'. Society garlic (3)

D *Anemone × hybrida* 'Prince Henry'. Japanese anemone (1)

E *Nandina domestica* 'Compacta'. Heavenly bamboo (9)

F *Artemisia* 'Powis Castle' (3)

G *Salvia leucantha*. Mexican bush sage (2)

H *Penstemon* 'Garnet'. Border penstemon (3)

I *Penstemon* 'Firebird'. Border penstemon (1)

J *Penstemon* 'Apple Blossom'. Border penstemon (1)

K *Alyogyne huegelii* 'Monterey Bay'. Blue hibiscus (1)

L *Buddleja davidii* 'Strawberry Lemonade'. Butterfly bush (1)

M *Stachys byzantina* 'Silver Carpet'. Lamb's ears (11)

N *Rosa*, Red Flower Carpet and Pink Flower Carpet, to fill

O *Rhaphiolepis indica*. Indian hawthorn (1)

P *Gladiolus* 'Firecracker' and 'Rapid Red' (2)

Planting area 15' x 25'

86

Planting area 28 x 12

plant list

A *Ribes sanguineum glutinosum* 'Spring Showers'. Pink winter currant (2)

B *Rhamnus californica* 'Mound San Bruno'. Coffeeberry (3)

C *Polystichum munitum.* Western sword fern (2)

D *Festuca californica.* California fescue (5)

E *Salvia spathacea.* Hummingbird sage (6)

F *Iris douglasiana.* Douglas iris (3)

G *Heuchera maxima.* Island alum root (6)

H *Asarum caudatum.* Wild ginger (4)

I *Satureja douglasii.* Yerba buena (5)

NATIVE WOODLANDS This lively collection of drought-tolerant plants native to the West Coast is well suited to a partly shaded spot, such as the edge of an oak woodland, in Zones 15–24. Coffeeberry and flowering currant create a backdrop for a simple bench flanked by ferns, grasses, and flowering perennials. Carpeting the area nearest the bench are yerba buena and wild ginger, both with highly fragrant leaves.

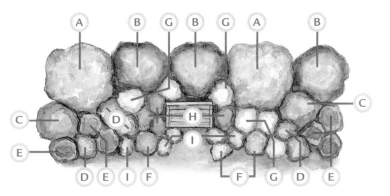

artful plot

tom's notebook

Set between a dark background of trees and a ribbon of deep green ornamental strawberry in front, this bright border composition was created around a gorgeous butter-yellow urn. Rather than trying to match the color exactly, the designer wisely chose variations on the yellow theme, with leaves in hues from cream to char- treuse and brilliant gold. The urn, though partly concealed by foliage, fairly shines.

The plants' textures also contrast beautifully. Notice how the large, sturdy-looking leaves of hosta and umbrella plant stand out against the slender, soft-appearing leaves of Japanese forest grass and lacy fern fronds.

Another interesting contrast exists between the two hard- scape elements: the smooth, glazed urn is elegant and upright; the dark stone birdbath is craggy and horizontal. Sitting side by side on a patio, they might look incongruous, but when surrounded by carefully chosen plants, they play off of each other beautifully.

Tom

1. Grass softens a rough edge and ties together the two hostas

2. Variegated plants are boldly grouped

3. A graceful, sweeping line is formed by stair-stepped plant heights

4. A water feature looks perfectly natural

This space is made for outdoor living, with a generously sized patio that allows a flexible mix of chairs and tables. Oversize square pavers zigzag through the lawn in a bold, graphic pattern that visually widens the narrow lot. Masses of spiky phormiums and agaves add to the strong design while billowing ornamental grasses round off the hard edges.

backyards

The backyard is where you can kick back and relax. When it comes to garden design, though, it can be a little overwhelming because the backyard is also the space that offers you the most opportunities. Do you want a serene retreat where you can sit quietly in the dappled shade, or do you lean more to an outdoor gathering place, with a patio, fireplace, and maybe even an outdoor kitchen? Will the yard showcase a collection of specimen plants, or be a playground for kids and pets? Do you even want a lawn, or would you prefer mulched paths winding among native plants? Or do you want all of the above?

The good news is that backyards need not be confined to one purpose or even have to function as a single space. With careful planning, you can find spaces for lounging, a vegetable garden, an outdoor kitchen and patio, and a kid's play space.

The garden plans we've included here offer a wide range of options, from ideas to fill smaller spaces, either on their own or within a larger landscape, to blueprints for a family garden. Pick and choose, or mix and mingle, until you find the design that's just right for your backyard.

A backyard lawn has been reinvented as a garden path, drawing the eye to the urn centered at the rear of the yard while serving as a foil to the plantings that line its edges.

FLORAL RETREAT This little garden makes use of pillowy perennials that will produce a colorful show the first season it's planted in Zones 4–9, 14–21, 29, 32–35 (in colder climates, the Santa Barbara daisy may not last). Flowers in fiery oranges, reds, and yellows are outlined with cool whites and grays.

plant list

A *Boltonia asteroides* 'Snowbank' (5)

B *Phygelius × rectus* 'Moonraker'. Cape fuchsia (4)

C *Chrysanthemum frutescens* 'Silver Leaf'. Marguerite (3)

D *Erodium corsicum* 'Album' (18)

E *Santolina chamaecyparissus* 'Compacta'. Lavender cotton (3)

F *Nemesia* 'Innocence' (3)

G *Penstemon* 'Firebird'. Border penstemon (5)

H *Rosa* 'Playboy' (1)

I *Rudbeckia hirta* 'Irish Eyes'. Gloriosa daisy (5)

J *Erigeron karvinskianus.* Santa Barbara daisy (4)

K *Thymus vulgaris* 'Argentus'. Silver thyme (4)

L *Veronica spicata* 'Icicle' (4)

M *Miscanthus sinensis.* Eulalia, Japanese silver grass (3)

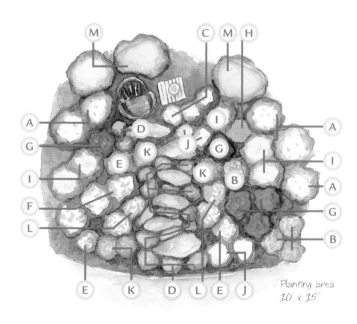

Planting area
10' × 15'

BREATHE DEEPLY Step into the garden, take a seat on the strategically placed bench, and inhale! This planting combines over a dozen famously fragrant perennials and shrubs—but you won't have to risk olfactory overload by trying to take in their varied perfumes all at once. Flowering starts with sweet violets in early spring, then progresses to lily-of-the-valley, lilac, mock orange, viburnum, and peony as the season advances. All these plants should thrive in Zones 2–6, 32–41, though the potted heliotrope will need winter shelter in a frost-free location.

plant list

A *Syringa vulgaris* 'President Lincoln'. Common lilac (1)

B *Viburnum carlesii*. Korean spice viburnum (1)

C *Clethra alnifolia*. Summersweet (2)

D *Philadelphus* 'Dwarf Minnesota Snowflake'. Mock orange (1)

E *Rosa rugosa* 'Rotes Meer' ('Purple Pavement') (2)

F *Paeonia* 'Edulis Superba'. Peony (2)

G *Dictamnus albus*. Gas plant (2)

H *Phlox paniculata* 'Eva Cullum'. Summer phlox (4)

I *Hemerocallis lilioasphodelus*. Lemon daylily (5)

J *Convallaria majalis*. Lily-of-the-valley (7)

K *Viola odorata*. Sweet violet (7)

L *Reseda odorata*. Mignonette (12)

M *Heliotropium arborescens*. Common heliotrope (1, in pot)

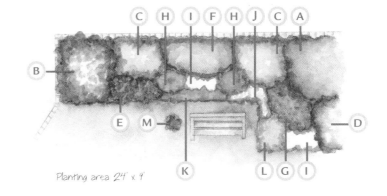

Planting area 24' x 9'

plant list

BACKYARD EDEN Though this space is only 30 feet by 40 feet, it offers the amenities of a large yard. There's an ample deck for lounging and entertaining, and enough lawn to provide play space for children and pets (and the occasional round of croquet). An orange or lemon tree satisfies that urge for home-grown produce; a compact rose garden promises plenty of flowers to enjoy both indoors and out. Finally, the view from the house is framed by plantings that remain attractive all year. The citrus tree identifies this plan as one for mild-winter regions: Zones 8, 9, 14–24.

A *Arbutus unedo.* Strawberry tree (1)

B *Feijoa sellowiana.* Pineapple guava (1)

C *Citrus* (orange or lemon) (1)

D *Rosa* 'Climbing Iceberg' (2)

E *Rosa,* hybrid tea (assorted) (6)

F *Escallonia* 'Compakta' (13)

G *Rhaphiolepis indica* 'White Enchantress'. Indian hawthorn (1)

H *Buxus microphylla japonica.* Japanese boxwood (18)

I *Lavatera thuringiaca* 'Barnsley'. Tree mallow (2)

J *Lavandula angustifolia.* English lavender (2)

K *Lantana* 'Dwarf Pink' (2)

L *Cistus* 'Doris Hibberson'. Rockrose (2)

M *Agastache* 'Tutti Frutti' (6)

N *Agapanthus* 'Storm Cloud'. Lily-of-the-Nile (6)

O *Dianthus gratianopolitanus* 'Little Joe'. Cheddar pink (12)

P *Erigeron karvinskianus.* Santa Barbara daisy (5)

Q *Teucrium cossonii majoricum.* Germander (5)

R *Osteospermum fruticosum.* Trailing African daisy (10)

S *Trachelospermum jasminoides.* Star jasmine (2, as ground cover)

T *Potentilla neumanniana.* Cinquefoil (20)

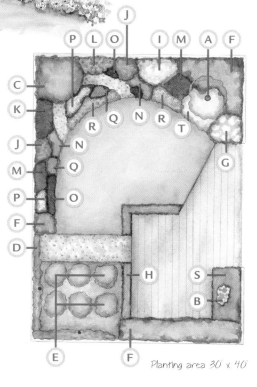

Planting area 30' x 40'

SPLIT-LEVEL GARDEN This group of three interlocking beds is adaptable to many a small yard. The two raised sections make it easy to tailor the planting scheme to suit your taste. Here, the raised-bed parts hold flowering perennials (suited to Zones 3–10, 14–24, 33), but they could just as well feature vegetables or herbs, leaving the ground-level bed free for seasonal color. Reverse the arrangement and you could have edible row crops at ground level, a cut-flower garden in the raised parts. This planting gives you color from late spring into fall, with a peak in early summer. To extend the plan into Zones 32, 34, and 35, use *Oenothera fruticosa* in place of the two Mexican evening primroses suggested under L and M in the list below.

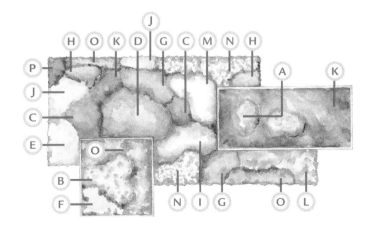

Planting area 20' x 10'

plant list

A *Gaura lindheimeri* (2)

B *Hemerocallis,* yellow cultivar. Daylily (3)

C *Perovskia atriplicifolia.* Russian sage (2)

D *Achillea millefolium,* Galaxy strain. Common yarrow (2)

E *Achillea* 'Moonshine'. Yarrow (1)

F *Achillea tomentosa.* Woolly yarrow (1)

G *Sedum* 'Autumn Joy'. Stonecrop (3)

H *Limonium platyphyllum.* Sea lavender (2)

I *Salvia officinalis* 'Purpurascens' ('Red Sage'). Common sage (2)

J *Coreopsis lanceolata* 'Goldfink' (3)

K *Nepeta* × *faassenii.* Catmint (7)

L *Oenothera speciosa* 'Siskiyou'. Mexican evening primrose (3)

M *Oenothera speciosa* 'Woodside White'. Mexican evening primrose (3)

N *Santolina chamaecyparissus.* Lavender cotton (3)

O *Stachys byzantina* 'Silver Carpet'. Lamb's ears (12)

P *Ceratostigma plumbaginoides.* Dwarf plumbago (1)

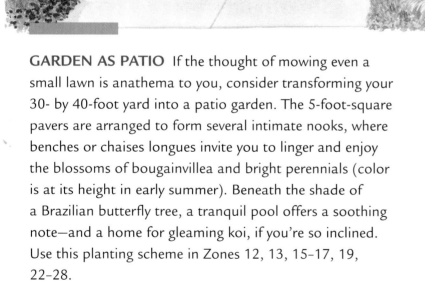

GARDEN AS PATIO If the thought of mowing even a small lawn is anathema to you, consider transforming your 30- by 40-foot yard into a patio garden. The 5-foot-square pavers are arranged to form several intimate nooks, where benches or chaises longues invite you to linger and enjoy the blossoms of bougainvillea and bright perennials (color is at its height in early summer). Beneath the shade of a Brazilian butterfly tree, a tranquil pool offers a soothing note—and a home for gleaming koi, if you're so inclined. Use this planting scheme in Zones 12, 13, 15–17, 19, 22–28.

plant list

A *Bougainvillea* 'California Gold' ('Sunset') (2)

B *Bougainvillea* 'Tahitian Dawn' (2)

C × *Fatshedera lizei* (1)

D *Bauhinia forficata.* Brazilian butterfly tree (1)

E *Yucca gloriosa.* Spanish dagger (1)

F *Osmanthus fragrans.* Sweet olive (3)

G *Feijoa sellowiana.* Pineapple guava (3)

H *Pittosporum tobira* 'Wheeler's Dwarf'. Tobira (11)

I *Punica granatum* 'Nana'. Dwarf pomegranate (7)

J *Abelia × grandiflora* 'Edward Goucher'. Glossy abelia (3)

K *Rhaphiolepis indica* 'Clara'. Indian hawthorn (2)

L *Dietes bicolor.* Fortnight lily (3)

M *Agapanthus praecox orientalis.* Lily-of-the-Nile (3)

N *Agapanthus* 'Peter Pan'. Lily-of-the-Nile (10)

O *Hemerocallis,* large yellow cultivar. Daylily (6)

P *Hemerocallis* 'Black-eyed Stella'. Daylily (5)

Q *Liriope muscari* 'Silvery Sunproof'. Big blue lily turf (9)

R *Ophiopogon japonicus.* Mondo grass (24)

S *Acanthus mollis.* Bear's breech (4)

T *Erigeron karvinskianus.* Santa Barbara daisy (15)

U *Achillea tomentosa* 'King George'. Woolly yarrow (14)

V *Verbena rigida* 'Flame' (7)

W *Verbena* 'Tapien Purple'. Moss verbena (20)

X *Ajuga reptans.* Carpet bugle (24)

Y *Teucrium × lucidrys* 'Prostratum'. Germander (22)

Z *Hedera helix* 'Glacier'. English ivy (12 starts)

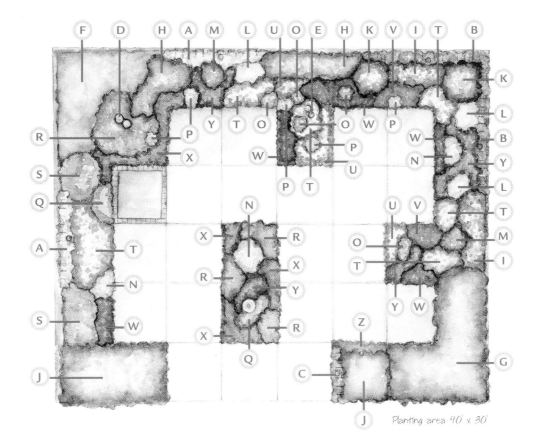

Planting area 40' x 30'

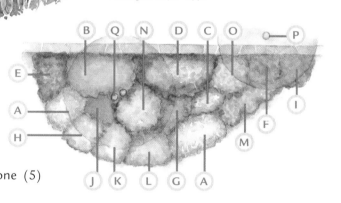

Planting area 28' × 11'

A CANOPY BED

Where two or more trees join forces to shelter an area, you can craft a fairly ambitious garden of shade-loving plants. Here, two garden-compatible trees—a locust and a dogwood—spread their limbs above a good-sized plot, casting mottled shadows over a diverse planting that sports variegated or colored foliage throughout the growing season and provides bursts of flower color from spring through fall. Both the plants and the two trees perform best with regular water, in Zones 4–9, 14, 15, 32.

plant list

A *Alchemilla mollis.*
Lady's-mantle (3)

B *Anemone × hybrida*
'Honorine Jobert'. Japanese anemone (5)

C *Molinia caerulea* 'Variegata'.
Moor grass (1)

D *Berberis thunbergii* 'Atropurpurea'.
Red-leaf Japanese barberry (2)

E *Bergenia crassifolia.*
Winter-blooming bergenia (3)

F *Digitalis purpurea.*
Common foxglove (4)

G *Helleborus argutifolius.*
Corsican hellebore (3)

H *Hosta* 'Chinese Sunrise'. Plantain lily (3)

I *Hosta sieboldiana* 'Elegans'.
Plantain lily (1)

J *Iris foetidissima.* Gladwin iris (2)

K *Lamium maculatum* 'White Nancy'.
Dead nettle (3)

L *Liriope muscari.* Big blue lily turf (3)

M *Liriope muscari* 'Variegata'.
Big blue lily turf (4)

N *Thalictrum aquilegiifolium.* Meadow rue (3)

O *Thalictrum rochebrunianum* 'Lavender Mist'.
Meadow rue (3)

P *Cornus × rutgersensis* 'Aurora'.
Stellar dogwood (1)

Q *Robinia pseudoacacia* 'Frisia'.
Black locust (1)

plant list

A *Styrax japonicus.*
Japanese snowdrop tree (5)

B *Solanum laxum.* Potato vine (8)

C *Rosa* 'Iceberg' (8)

D *Hydrangea macrophylla* (white and pink varieties). Bigleaf hydrandea (4)

E *Lavandula angustifolia.*
English lavender (8)

F *Nepeta × faassenii.* Catmint (11)

G *Anemone × hybrida* 'Alba' .
Japanese anemone (12)

H *Pittosporum tenuifolium*
'Silver Sheen' (2)

I *Delphinium elatum.*
Candle delphinium (purple) (2)

J *Camellia japonica* 'Purity' (2)

K *Viola × wittrockiana* (white).
Pansy (6)

URBAN OASIS This city garden has it all—patio, grass, flowering shrubs, and even a water feature. It's proof positive that small spaces can still deliver a big impact. The shrubs along the back provide color and screen the yard from neighboring windows. Closer to the house, a semi-circular patio breaks up the straight lines found in the rest of the garden. Designed for Zone 17, this garden will do well in Zones 8, 9, 14–21.

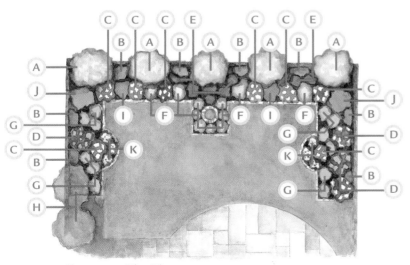

Planting area 36' x 24'

Planting area 20' x 16'

plant list

A *Aruncus dioicus.* Goat's beard (2)

B *Alchemilla mollis.* Lady's-mantle (8+)

C *Hakonechloa macra* 'Aureola'. Japanese forest grass (4)

D *Helleborus orientalis.* Lenten rose (6+)

E *Brunnera macrophylla.* Brunnera (8+)

F *Thalictrum aquilegiifolium.* Meadow rue (3)

G *Corydalis lutea* (6+)

H *Astilbe simplicifolia* 'Sprite'. False spirea (5)

I *Athyrium filix-femina.* Lady fern (2)

J *Galax urceolata* (4)

K *Hosta* 'Gold Edger'. Plantain lily (10+)

L *Hyacinthoides non-scripta.* English bluebell (16)

VENERABLE SHELTER Though a mature deciduous tree is a treasure to be cherished, it often sits squarely in a spot where you'd also like to establish an ornamental planting. Some trees, such as sweet gum *(Liquidambar),* have aggressive surface root systems that will ultimately defeat your efforts. But given a reasonably deep-rooted tree like the scarlet oak *(Quercus coccinea)* shown here, you can literally have it all. The limbs extend to shelter a potpourri of shade-tolerant plants that reach a crescendo of color in summer, brightening the garden with both flowers and non-green foliage. These plants will succeed in Zones 3–6, 32–41.

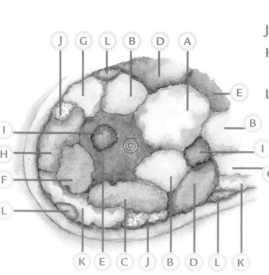

DRY-SHADE DENIZENS Shade and dryness characterize the conditions of many a forest floor, where the typical flora features plenty of greenery and few or no blossoms. The same basic scheme holds true in dry, low-light garden spots. This planting adorns the ground beneath a Japanese pagoda tree *(Sophora japonica)*. The variegated leaves of Japanese aucuba, osmanthus, and lily turf add light to the composition; red tints in the foliage of heavenly bamboo and bishop's hat contribute a touch of color. Notable flower color comes just from lily turf, bishop's hat, and cinquefoil. Use this grouping in Zones 4–9, 14–17, 32, and 33. Gardeners in Zones 10, 18–21 can substitute dwarf periwinkle *(Vinca minor)* for bishop's hat (G in the list below).

Planting area 35 × 12

plant list

A *Aucuba japonica* 'Picturata'.
Japanese aucuba (2)

B *Osmanthus heterophyllus* 'Variegatus'.
Holly-leaf osmanthus (3)

C *Mahonia aquifolium* 'Compacta'. Oregon grape (12)

D *Nandina domestica* 'Harbor Dwarf'.
Heavenly bamboo (9+)

E *Iris foetidissima.* Gladwin iris (5)

F *Liriope muscari* 'Silvery Sunproof'. Big blue lily turf (7)

G *Epimedium* × *rubrum* (10)

H *Potentilla recta* 'Warrenii'. Cinquefoil (4)

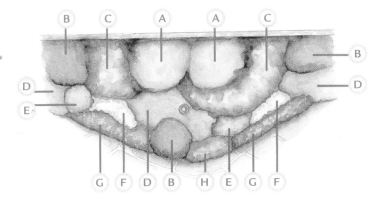

plant list

A *Rosmarinus officinalis* 'Prostratus'. Rosemary (1)

B *Lavandula angustifolia* 'Hidcote'. English lavender (9)

C *Iris,* Siberian (3)

D *Nepeta* 'Six Hills Giant'. Catmint (3)

E *Rosa* (2)

F *Viburnum × burkwoodii* (2)

G *Parthenocissus quinquefolia.* Virginia creeper (1)

H *Sedum* 'Autumn Joy'. Stonecrop (5)

I *Spiraea japonica* 'Anthony Waterer'. Spirea (3)

J *Zantedeschia aethiopica.* Common calla (1)

K *Choisya ternata.* Mexican orange (3)

L *Malus* 'Dolgo'. Flowering crabapple (1)

M *Heuchera sanguinea.* Coral bells (5)

QUIET CORNER Even if your yard backs up to a busy street, it can still become a quiet retreat. Here's a great example: deep garden beds filled with deep reds and greens, plus dark red Virginia creeper masking the fence turn this space into a calm and inviting sanctuary from the world just outside. Undulating garden bed edgings keep the space from being too regimented. The garden works well in Zones 6–9, 14–24; the ideas can be incorporated into any yard.

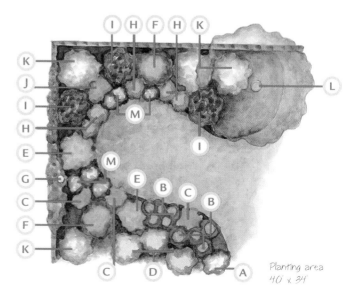

Planting area 40' x 34'

A GRASSY GLADE This design includes some easy-care plants to make it a truly stress-free retreat in Zones 3–9, 14–17, though many of these plants will do well in colder areas. Evergreens and a fence along the garden's perimeter provide privacy while flowering vines on a trellis mask the view to a service area. The changes in elevation from the step-down patio make the garden appear larger. Other interesting touches: natural stones in the planting beds, an accent sculpture, and a recirculating waterfall spilling into a tranquil pool.

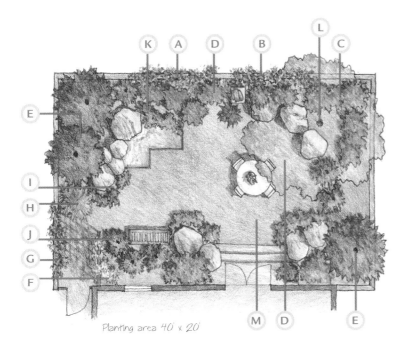

Planting area 40' × 20'

plant list

A *Berberis koreana.* Korean barberry (3)

B *Campsis × tagliabuana* 'Mme Galen'. Trumpet vine (2)

C *Diervilla lonicera.* Bush honeysuckle (3)

D *Helictotrichon sempervirens.* Blue oat grass (3)

E *Juniperus chinensis* 'Obelisk'. Chinese juniper (3)

F *Lonicera japonica* 'Halliana'. Japanese honeysuckle (1)

G *Lonicera sempervirens* 'John Clayton'. Trumpet honeysuckle (1)

H *Miscanthus sinensis* 'Kleine Silberspinne'. Eulalia, Japanese silver grass (1)

I *Pachysandra terminalis* 'Green Carpet'. Japanese spurge (6)

J *Pinus mugo.* Mugho pine (3)

K *Sedum* 'Autumn Joy', *S. telephium.* Stonecrop (5)

L *Syringa reticulata* 'Ivory Silk'. Japanese tree lilac (1)

M Kentucky bluegrass mix

personal paradise | creating a tranquil backyard

Even the smallest backyard can have space for a lawn, planting beds, and a path to connect them. The trick is to make all of these spaces work together. In this garden, a curving gravel path encircles the center lawn and links the house with the planting beds and the patio to the right. Lush beds of low-maintenance perennials soften the edges and open up the view.

Antique trellises on the walls of the house help break up the stark expanse—and give the garden the feel of an old-world courtyard.

A dry-stacked stone wall forms the border of a raised planting bed, which in turn gives the flat garden a gentle hint of height and provides additional visual interest.

plant list

A *Pelargonium tomentosum*. Peppermint geranium

B *Nandina domestica*. Heavenly bamboo

C *Thymus vulgaris* 'Argenteus'. Silver thyme

D *Sedum* 'Autumn Joy'. Stonecrop

E *Pennisetum orientale* 'Karley Rose'. Fountain grass

F *Zinnia elegans* 'Peter Pan Cream'

G *Thymus pseudolanuginosus*. Woolly thyme

H *Sedum spurium*. Stonecrop

I *Geranium incanum* 'Sugar Plum'. Cranesbill

A FAMILY GARDEN Trying to fit a range of family interests (seating, dining, play areas, a pool or spa, and both flower and vegetable beds) into a single garden might seem an impossible task. But this garden, at 55 by 65 feet, proves it can be done. The secret lies in judiciously placing the hardscape elements, such as the pool, patio area, and play structure, and relying on a relatively small selection of plants to provide continuity throughout. Families in Zones 8-9, 14-24, 25, and 28 can all use this design, and many of the plants will do well in Zones 29-31.

Agapanthus 'Peter Pan'

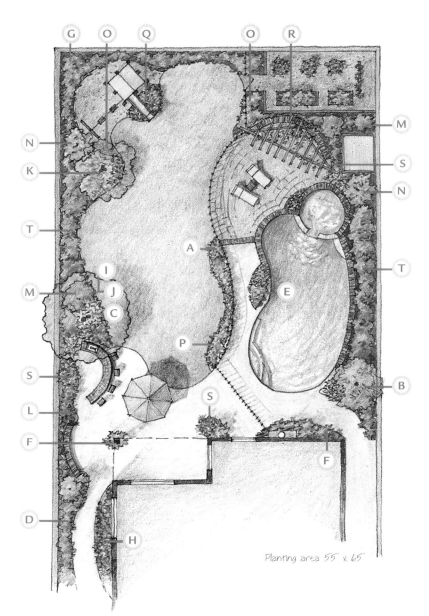

Planting area 55' x 65'

plant list

A *Agapanthus praecox orientalis.* Lily-of-the-Nile (2)

B *Arbutus unedo.* Strawberry tree (1)

C *Cinnamomum camphora.* Camphor tree (1)

D *Citrus.* 'Improved Meyer' lemon (1)

E *Coprosma repens* 'Marble Queen'. Mirror plant (3)

F *Distictis buccinatoria.* Blood-red trumpet vine (2)

G *Ficus microcarpa nitida.* Indian laurel fig (1)

H *Herbs*

I *Heuchera sanguinea.* Coral bells (6)

J *Iris* (5)

K *Jacaranda mimosifolia* (1)

L *Limonium perezii.* Sea lavender (5)

M *Pittosporum tobira* 'Variegata'. Tobira (1)

N *Rhaphiolepis* 'Majestic Beauty' (1)

O *Soleirolia soleirolii.* Baby's tears (6)

P *Trachelospermum jasminoides.* Star jasmine (7)

Q *Vinca minor.* Dwarf periwinkle (3)

R *Wisteria sinensis.* Chinese wisteria (1)

S *Woodwardia fimbriata.* Giant chain fern (1)

T *Xylosma congestum* (8)

Limonium perezii   *Xylosma congestum*

plant list

A *Brugmansia.* Angel's trumpet (2)

B *Buddleja davidii.* Butterfly bush (1)

C *Penstemon* 'Midnight'.
Border penstemon (3)

D *Origanum.* Variegated oregano (6)

E *Pennisetum setaceum* 'Rubrum'.
Fountain grass (2)

F *Tibouchina heteromalla* (1)

G *Pittosporum tobira* 'Wheeler's
Dwarf'. Tobira (2)

H *Osteospermum fruticosum.*
Trailing African daisy (1)

I *Solanum rantonnetii* (1)

J *Verbena × hybrida.*
Garden verbena (6)

K *Lavandula angustifolia.*
English lavender (1)

L *Nassella tenuissima.*
Mexican feather grass (1)

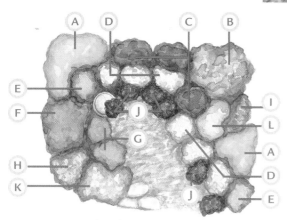

Planting area 10' x 10'

A NEW VIEW What can you do with a bare spot in a highly visible corner of the backyard? Create a view garden, like this textural planting. This garden already had feather grass and a mature buddleja, so the designer added more purple-flowered plants, plus variegated oregano for a spritz of lime. To add some graceful motion, the choice was purple fountain grass. The plants are layered around the main focal point—an old pot brought back to life with a coat of lime green paint and filled with purple verbena. This garden does well in Zones 8–24; in colder climates, grow the frost-tender plants as annuals or in big pots you can move to a protected spot for winter.

Planting area 7' x 24'

plant list

A *Achillea millefolium,* Galaxy strain, pink selection. Common yarrow (2)

B *Achillea* 'Moonshine'. Yarrow (2)

C *Arabis caucasica.* Wall rockcress (1)

D *Berberis thunbergii* 'Atropurpurea'. Red-leaf Japanese barberry (1)

E *Buxus microphylla koreana.* Korean boxwood (8)

F *Clematis* 'Henryi' (2)

G *Dianthus plumarius.* Cottage pink (3)

H *Baptisia alba.* White false indigo (1)

I *Echinacea purpurea.* Purple coneflower (9)

J *Hemerocallis* 'Little Grapette'. Daylily (5)

K *Iris,* Siberian, 'Caesar's Brother' (6)

L *Lagerstroemia indica,* pink cultivar. Crape myrtle (1)

M *Lavandula angustifolia.* English lavender (3)

N *Liatris spicata* 'Kobold'. Gayfeather (4)

O *Nepeta × faassenii.* Catmint (5)

P *Rosa* 'Heritage' (1)

Q *Rosa* 'White Pet' (1)

R *Rosa* 'New Dawn' (1)

S *Salvia × sylvestris* 'May Night'. Sage (4)

T *Sedum* 'Autumn Joy'. Stonecrop (7)

U *Spiraea japonica* 'Limemound'. Spirea (1)

V *Spiraea japonica* 'Little Princess'. Spirea (1)

W *Stachys byzantina* 'Silver Carpet'. Lamb's ears (4)

A THREE-SEASON GARDEN MEDLEY

From spring through fall, this garden's wrought-iron bench offers a prime vantage point for admiring the shifting colors of perennials, shrubs, and graceful crape myrtle. The illustration shows the planting in its early-summer dress, when the rockcress, daylily, cottage pink, and iris have already finished their bloom and the sedum and crape myrtle have yet to flower. Throughout the three growing seasons, you'll enjoy consistent non-green foliage color from the barberry, 'Moonshine' yarrow, lavender, sedum, 'Limemound' spirea, and lamb's ears. This pleasant potpourri is available to gardeners in Zones 7–9, 14, and 31.

A GARDEN FOR ALL SEASONS In a northern climate with well-defined seasons, it makes sense to plan the garden to showcase natural displays during every season. In this garden, plants were chosen for their bright flowers, fruit, seeds, foliage color, interesting bark, or other contrasts of texture during specific times of the year. In winter, the winged stems of the burning bush and the textured bark of the river birch stand out in the snow. Spring brings bulbs in bloom, the yellow catkins of the filbert, and yellow spiderlike blooms of witch hazel. Visitors can sit on the bench and absorb the sights and scents of summer with pleasure, while fall brings brilliant color. This garden was designed for Zones 1–9, 32–45.

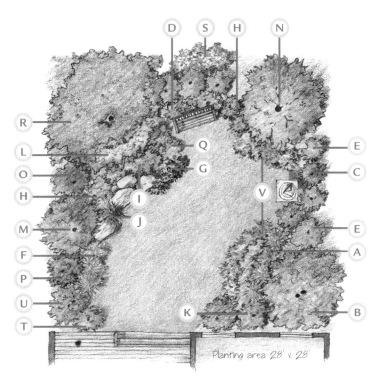

Planting area 28' x 28'

plant list

A *Andropogon gerardii.* Big bluestem (5)

B *Betula nigra* 'Heritage'. River birch (2)

C *Corylus americana.* American hazelnut (1)

D *Euonymus alatus* 'Compacta'. Winged euonymus (5)

E *Hamamelis virginiana.* Common witch hazel (2)

F *Helictotrichon sempervirens.* Blue oat grass (3)

G *Heuchera* 'Chocolate Ruffles'. Purple alum root (7)

H *Hosta sieboldiana* 'Elegans'. Plantain lily (3)

I *Juniperus sabina* 'Broadmoor'. Savin juniper (1)

J *Miscanthus sinensis* 'Purpurascens'. Flame grass (1)

K *Myrica pensylvanica.* Bayberry (2)

L *Pachysandra terminalis* 'Green Carpet'. Japanese spurge (4)

M *Pinus densiflora* 'Umbraculifera'. Tanyosho pine (1)

N *Pinus resinosa.* Red pine (1)

O *Rhododendron* 'Boule de Neige' (1)

P *Rhododendron (azalea)* 'Pink and Sweet' (1)

Q *Sedum* 'Autumn Joy'. Stonecrop (5)

R *Sorbus americana.* American mountain ash (1)

S *Syringa vulgaris* 'Miss Ellen Willmott'. Common lilac (double white) (2)

T *Thuja occidentalis* 'Caespitosa'. American arborvitae (2)

U *Viburnum trilobum* 'Compactum'. American cranberry bush (2)

V Bulbs: *Colchicum autumnale* 'Roseum Plenum', Autumn crocus; *Narcissus* 'Dutch Master', Daffodil; *Tulipa* 'Apricot Beauty', tulip

Perennials: *Aster ericoides* 'Pink Cloud' (7); *Coreopsis verticillata* 'Moonbeam' (7)

plant list

A *Salix integra* 'Hakuro Nishiki'. Dappled willow (1)

B *Betula pendula.* European white birch (2)

C *Ligustrum japonicum.* Japanese privet (hedge) (7)

D *Hemerocallis* hybrids. Evergreen daylily (5)

E *Hydrangea macrophylla.* Bigleaf hydrangea (2)

F *Canna,* red-leafed and green-leafed hybrids (4)

G *Salix babylonica pekinensis* 'Tortuosa'. Dragon-claw willow (1)

H *Rudbeckia fulgida sullivantii* 'Goldsturm' (2)

I *Calamagrostis × acutiflora* 'Karl Foerster'. Feather reed grass (9)

J *Phyllostachys aurea.* Golden bamboo (as hedge)

K *Carex albula* 'Frosted Curls'. Sedge (7)

L *Chamaemelum nobile.* Chamomile (12)

M *Festuca glauca.* Common blue fescue (12)

N *Festuca rubra.* Red fescue (40 plugs)

O *Lobularia maritima* 'Violet Queen'. Sweet alyssum (7)

P *Salvia elegans.* Pineapple sage (1)

Q *Carex buchananii.* Leather leaf sedge (7)

R *Astilbe chinensis.* False spirea (3)

MEADOW MAGIC When maintaining a traditional lawn is a struggle, why not turn to a low-maintenance substitute? This backyard meadow is filled with fragrant chamomile, low-growing sedges, and fine-textured sedges. The grasses need occasional shearing, but their colors and textures blend to create a naturally shaggy ground cover. Daylilies pop up like wayside wildflowers, and self-sufficient perennials are planted here and there around the edges. The final touch is a quietly bubbling fountain in one corner. These plants do well in Zones 6–7, 14–24.

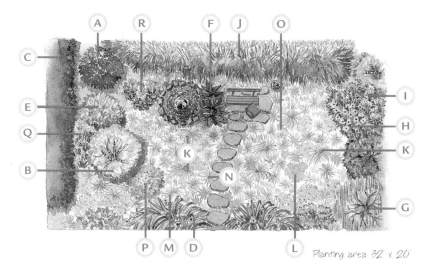

Planting area 32' x 20'

LOW-MAINTENANCE MASTERPIECE Unique to this three-season planting is its composition: all the plants are shrubby, from shrubby perennials through true shrubs to a magnolia that blurs the boundary between shrub and tree. The flowering year begins with the magnolia's waxy purple-and-white blossoms, then carries on with the springtime assortment of bloom shown here. And throughout the seasons, you'll have constant foliage interest from leaves in shades of yellow, bronze, and soft gray. Try this combination in Zones 4–6, 14–17, 32, 34.

plant list

A *Abelia × grandiflora* 'Sherwoodii'. Glossy abelia (1)

B *Berberis thunbergii* 'Cherry Bomb'. Japanese barberry (1)

C *Buddleja davidii* 'Black Knight'. Butterfly bush (1)

D *Caryopteris × clandonensis* 'Worcester Gold'. Blue mist (1)

E *Ceratostigma plumbaginoides*. Dwarf plumbago (3)

F *Erysimum* 'Bowles Mauve'. Wallflower (1)

G *Genista lydia*. Broom (2)

H *Lavandula angustifolia*. English lavender (3)

I *Lavandula angustifolia* 'Munstead'. English lavender (2)

J *Lonicera × heckrottii*. Goldflame honeysuckle (1)

K *Magnolia* 'Randy' (1)

L *Nandina domestica* 'Woods Dwarf'. Heavenly bamboo (3)

M *Potentilla* 'Katherine Dykes'. Cinquefoil (2)

N *Rosa* 'Fair Bianca' (1)

O *Rosa* 'New Dawn' (1)

P *Salvia officinalis* 'Berggarten'. Common sage (2)

Q *Santolina chamaecyparissus* 'Nana'. Lavender cotton (3)

R *Spiraea japonica* 'Limemound'. Spirea (2)

S *Teucrium × lucidrys* 'Prostratum'. Germander (5)

T *Thymus pseudolanuginosus*. Woolly thyme (between paving stones)

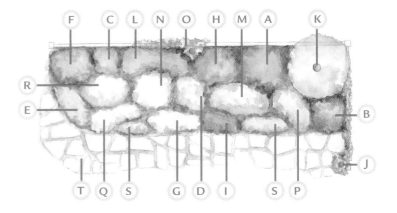

Planting area 24' x 8'

Planting area 9' x 20'

THREE SEASONS OF FLOWERS A varied assortment of annuals, perennials, and one red rose keeps the bouquets coming from spring to frost. Not everything will be flowering at once, of course, but even the out-of-bloom plants present an attractively leafy appearance. This garden needs a bit of winter chill, and is intended for Zones 1–9, 14–16, 18–21, 32–41. By substituting *Chrysanthemum* × *rubellum* 'Clara Curtis' for *Coreopsis rosea* (L) and *Aster novae-angliae* 'Alma Pötschke' for *Aster* × *frikartii* 'Mönch' (M), you can enjoy the garden in Zones 42–43, although the 'Mister Lincoln' rose will need winter protection.

plant list

A *Rosa* 'Mister Lincoln' (1)

B *Gypsophila paniculata.* Baby's breath (2)

C *Paeonia* (herbaceous), pink cultivar. Peony (1)

D *Chrysanthemum maximum.* Shasta daisy (3)

E *Alcea rosea,* Chater's Double strain. Hollyhock (6)

F *Physostegia virginiana* 'Variegata'. False dragonhead (1)

G *Psylliostachys suworowii* (3)

H *Aquilegia,* Music strain. Columbine (2)

I *Scabiosa caucasica.* Pincushion flower (3)

J *Heuchera sanguinea.* Coral bells (2)

K *Iberis sempervirens* 'Autumn Snow'. Evergreen candytuft (3)

L *Coreopsis rosea* (3)

M *Aster* × *frikartii* 'Mönch' (2)

N *Zinnia elegans* 'Candy Stripe' (4)

O *Antirrhinum majus,* Rocket or Topper strain. Snapdragon (4)

P *Cosmos bipinnatus* 'Picotee' (6)

Q *Nicotiana alata,* Domino strain. Flowering tobacco (6)

R *Tagetes erecta,* Sweet Cream strain. African marigold (6)

S *Viola* × *wittrockiana.* Pansy (3)

T *Gomphrena globosa.* Globe amaranth (5)

WARM-CLIMATE COLOR This design mirrors the garden on the facing page, but the choice of plants makes it very different. The 'Mister Lincoln' rose (A) is a common element, but nearly all else has changed, selected to suit warmer-winter climates. Though about a third of the plants will survive sub-zero winters, the group as a whole does best in Zones 6–9, 14–24. The Transvaal daisy (G) is hardy only in Zones 8–9; the sea lavender (M) is perennial only in frostless and nearly frost-free climes.

Planting area 4' x 20'

plant list

A *Rosa* 'Mister Lincoln' (1)

B *Penstemon* 'Holly's White'. Border penstemon (3)

C *Euphorbia characias wulfenii* (1)

D *Echinacea purpurea* 'Bravado'. Purple coneflower (2)

E *Centranthus ruber*. Jupiter's beard (2)

F *Achillea millefolium,* Garden Pastels strain. Common yarrow (2)

G *Gerbera jamesonii,* flame red cultivar. Transvaal daisy (2)

H *Chrysanthemum* × *grandiflorum,* bronze pompon type. Florists' chrysanthemum (3)

I *Coreopsis grandiflora* 'Sunray' (2)

J *Dianthus* 'Allwoodii'. Pink (2)

K *Sedum* 'Autumn Joy'. Stonecrop (1)

L *Scabiosa columbaria*. Pincushion flower (2)

M *Limonium perezii*. Sea lavender (1)

N *Achillea* × *taygetea*. Yarrow (2)

O *Iberis sempervirens* 'Autumn Snow'. Evergreen candytuft (3)

P *Linaria purpurea*. Toadflax (4)

Q *Tagetes erecta,* Sweet Cream strain. African marigold (4)

R *Calendula offinalis,* cream-colored cultivar (2)

S *Papaver nudicaule*. Iceland poppy (2)

T *Celosia* 'Apricot Brandy'. Plume cockscomb (6)

casual and colorful

tom's notebook

This casual backyard, very much in the cottage-garden style, is far more appealing to me than a traditional lawn surrounded by flower beds. Though the design has a relaxed look, it shows a carefully planned color scheme of reds and pinks highlighted by purple and white. The gravel chosen for the path blends the colors of the house with those of the painted shed, and an old olive jar serves as a rustic focal point that picks up on those same hues. I especially like the concrete sphere—moveable garden art. Rather than covering the garden shed with a trellis or clinging vine, the gardeners use it as a backdrop for dramatic spires of hollyhock.

There are plenty of places to sit in this garden, but none is set in stone. An old folding chair halfway down the path is right in line with the casual feel, and it must come in handy for jobs like deadheading.

Tom

1 Plants are layered from short in front to tall in back

2 A simple arch puts the focus on the roses, not the structure

3 Verbena spills onto the path, concealing the olive jar's base

4 Chairs placed along the path invite visitors to sit, relax, and enjoy the view

themes
and variations

specialty gardens ❧ flower gardens ❧ plantings plus ❧ color gardens

Palms, ferns, grasses, and other plants with junglelike foliage have turned this backyard into a tropical oasis. The mix of dramatic plants and rich colors is key to this look; even in less-than-tropical climates, choosing similar plants will help create the same effect. The addition of a tiki-inspired shelter and bamboo furniture is the finishing touch.

specialty gardens

Selecting a garden style is similar to choosing a personal style. Basically it depends on your individual likes and dislikes. You may find yourself sticking to the old-fashioned tried-and-true favorites, fascinated by the world of tropicals and tropical look-alikes, or drawn to the new ornamental grasses that are becoming more readily available. But don't forget the best gardens complement the architecture of the houses with which they're paired.

This doesn't mean that you're limited to only one look for your home. With the right plants, a garden filled with ornamental grasses can look right at home with a 19th-century Victorian, and the cottage garden lover with a 20th-century-modern house can still fill the yard with billowing flowers. The secret is to choose plants with colors and shapes that relate to their surroundings.

These 17 gardens run the gamut from traditional to contemporary. You'll find a side yard with an Asian influence, a tropical paradise, a southwestern-style garden, and a backyard prairie design. Note also the ideas for water gardens, rock gardens, and a planting of succulents. No matter what look you want, you'll find something that captures your interest—and style.

A rustic bench is the destination for a stroll through this woodlands garden. Though the color scheme is monochromatic and the emphasis is on foliage rather than flowers, the wide-ranging shades of green keep the garden interesting.

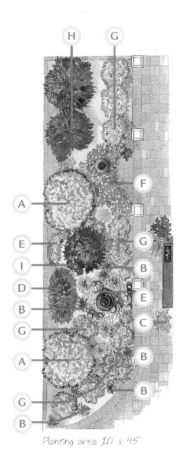

Planting area 10' x 45'

FOCUS ON A FOUNTAIN An Asian jar, found at a garden shop and transformed into a fountain, is the focal point of this narrow yard filled with a collection of shade-loving plants. Add some carefully placed rocks, an aged brick wall for privacy, and a Chinese red bench for contemplating it all, and the result is a cool green retreat highlighted by a brief moment of color each spring, courtesy of the azaleas. Designed for Zone 16, this garden will generally do well in Zones 4–9, 14–17, although the maidenhair fern is tender.

plant list

A *Acer circinatum.* Vine maple (2)

B *Liriope muscari.* Big blue lily turf (6)

C *Adiantum raddianum.* Maidenhair fern (6)

D *Fatsia japonica.* Japanese aralia (1)

E *Tiarella* 'Iron Butterfly'. Foamflower (3)

F *Helleborus* hybrids. Hellebore (5)

G *Rhododendron (azalea),* pink varieties (10)

H *Laurus nobilis.* Sweet bay (2)

I *Acer palmatum.* Japanese maple (1)

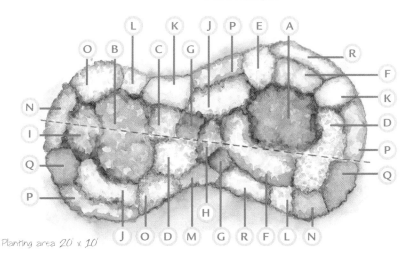

NORTH STAR The long, cold winters of higher latitudes and altitudes do limit the variety of plants you can grow, but they put no limits on garden beauty. The planting shown here provides a confettilike cascade of harmonious flower colors from late spring through summer. Foliage is only slightly less varied, featuring leaves in gray as well as green, with an assortment of textures. The full design is an island, but you can split it into two plans for use against a fence or walk; divide it along the dotted line. The planting is suitable for the coldest zones as well as more temperate regions, succeeding in Zones 1–9, 14–16, 32–45.

Planting area 20' x 10'

plant list

A *Rosa* 'Jens Munk' (1)

B *Paeonia,* pink cultivar. Peony (2)

C *Campanula persicifolia.* Peach-leafed bluebell (2)

D *Gypsophila paniculata* 'Perfecta'. Baby's breath (3)

E *Gypsophila paniculata* 'Viette's Dwarf' or 'Compacta Plena'. Baby's breath (2)

F *Achillea* 'Moonshine'. Yarrow (6)

G *Iris,* Siberian, 'Caesar's Brother' (3)

H *Liatris spicata.* Gayfeather (3)

I *Liatris spicata* 'Kobold'. Gayfeather (4)

J *Hemerocallis* 'Happy Returns'. Daylily (7)

K *Oenothera fruticosa* 'Fireworks'. Sundrops (5)

L *Euphorbia polychroma* (2)

M *Heuchera* × *brizoides,* pink cultivar. Coral bells (4)

N *Heuchera sanguinea.* Coral bells (10)

O *Iberis sempervirens* 'Snowflake'. Evergreen candytuft (3)

P *Dianthus* 'Allwoodii', pink cultivar. Pink (12)

Q *Phlox subulata,* lavender cultivar. Moss pink (3)

R *Artemisia schmidtiana* 'Silver Mound'. Angel's hair (7)

STRICTLY SOUTHWEST One of the advantages of gardening in Southwestern Zones 12–24 is the mild winter, which favors a great variety of plants. On the down side, though, are the dry conditions that prevail over much of the territory for a good portion of the year. No wonder, then, that plantings thriving on just moderate moisture are highly favored in these zones. When you choose the plan shown here, you can trade hauling the hose for reclining on the chaise to soak up some sun.

plant list

A *Rhaphiolepis* 'Majestic Beauty' (multitrunked) (1)

B *Leucophyllum frutescens.* Texas ranger (1)

C *Nerium oleander* 'Petite Salmon'. Oleander (2)

D *Lavandula × intermedia* 'Provence'. Lavandin (2)

E *Salvia leucantha.* Mexican bush sage (2)

F *Gaura lindheimeri* (2)

G *Artemisia* 'Powis Castle' (2)

H *Penstemon* 'Firebird'. Border penstemon (4)

I *Penstemon* 'Appleblossom'. Border penstemon (4)

J *Agapanthus* 'Queen Anne'. Lily-of-the-Nile (4)

K *Dietes iridioides.* Fortnight lily (1)

L *Santolina chamaecyparissus.* Lavender cotton (1)

M *Convolvulus cneorum.* Bush morning glory (1)

N *Convolvulus sabatius.* Ground morning glory (2)

O *Verbena peruviana* (4)

P *Gaillardia × grandiflora* 'Goblin Yellow'. Blanket flower (3)

Q *Gazania,* mixed colors (8)

R *Cistus* 'Victor Reiter'. Rockrose (1)

S *Cistus laurifolius.* Rockrose (1)

T *Cistus* 'Doris Hibberson'. Rockrose (1)

U *Cistus salviifolius.* Sageleaf rockrose (2)

V *Cistus* 'Sunset'. Rockrose (2)

W *Cistus* 'Warley Rose'. Rockrose (1)

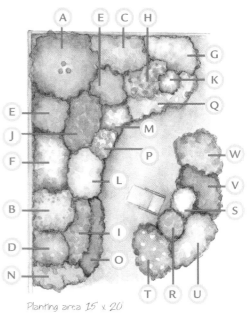

Planting area 15' × 20'

plant list

A *Brugmansia × candida.* Angel's trumpet (1)

B *Tibouchina urvilleana.* Princess flower (1)

C *Hibiscus rosa-sinensis* 'Fiesta' or 'Ross Estey'. Chinese hibiscus (1)

D *Mandevilla* 'Alice du Pont' (1)

E *Brunfelsia pauciflora* 'Macrantha' (1)

F *Justicia brandegeeana.* Shrimp plant (2)

G *Cuphea ignea.* Cigar plant (5)

H *Phygelius × rectus* 'African Queen'. Cape fuchsia (2)

I *Hemerocallis* (evergreen), yellow cultivar. Daylily (6+)

J *Liriope muscari* 'Silvery Sunproof'. Big blue lily turf (14)

K *Clivia miniata* (9)

L *Zantedeschia aethiopica.* Common calla (2)

M *Colocasia esculenta* 'Black Magic'. Taro, elephant's ear (2)

N *Hedychium gardnerianum.* Kahili ginger (3)

O *Chlorophytum comosum* 'Variegatum' or 'Vittatum'. Spider plant (12)

P *Pentas lanceolata.* Star clusters (4)

Q *Impatiens,* New Guinea hybrid, 'Tango' (3)

R *Zoysia tenuifolia.* Korean grass (sprigs or plugs, set 6 inches apart)

S *Gardenia agusta* 'White Gem' (1)

T *Caladium bicolor* 'White Queen'. Fancy-leafed caladium (3)

U *Solenostemon scutellarioides.* Coleus (3)

BICOASTAL TROPICS You're not in Kansas anymore. This is Honolulu...or Miami...or San Diego, where frost is a stranger and tropical luxuriance is the norm. The plant assortment shown here is still tough enough to weather the occasional slight frost, making it suitable to Zones 24–27. Prominent are two signature plants of tropic climes: kahili ginger and taro, or elephant's ear.

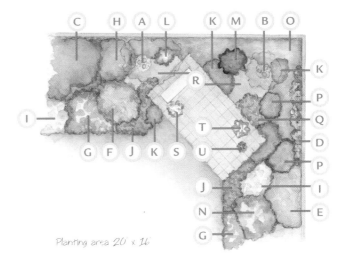

Planting area 20' x 16'

tropical twist | new look for a neglected space

A neglected space took a turn for the tropics when the owners decided to rescue the narrow (18- by 70-foot) space and turn it into a new outdoor living area. This gently sloping hillside is now home to a two-tiered flagstone patio flanked by garden beds filled with big, bold plants. The dining patio was set at a 45-degree angle to the house, which helps make the narrow space feel wider. Planting beds are only about 3 feet wide, but packing them with plants makes them seem deeper.

Bold architecture calls for bold plants, and the choices here provide plenty of dramatic foliage and intense color, primarily in vibrant shades of red, orange, and yellow.

Specimen plants like this statuesque banana, seen against the white stucco walls of the house, function almost as works of art.

plant list

A *Brugmansia cubensis* 'Charles Grimaldi'. Angel's trumpet

B *Begonia,* tuberous

C *Canna* 'Tropicanna'

D *Abutilon,* orange hybrid. Flowering maple

E *Phormium* hybrid

F *Musa,* Ornamental banana

G *Dahlia,* red, informal decorative form

H *Ajuga reptans* 'Catlin's Giant'. Carpet bugle

THE PLOT THICKENS A too-small and somewhat scraggly vegetable garden
was transformed into an exuberant flower garden, complete with a flagstone
path around it and a sitting area to the side. The flowers shown here do well in
Zones 1–10, 14–16, 18–21, 32, 34, 36–41, but you can adapt this plan to
showcase any annuals and perennials that thrive in your own climate. To keep
things in check, a border of willow branches surrounds the space, and longer
willow sticks make a 4-foot tepee for the bright pink morning glories.

*Thymus
pseudolanuginosus*

plant list

A *Gypsophila paniculata.* Baby's breath (2)

B *Rudbeckia fulgida sullivantii* 'Goldsturm' (3)

C *Cosmos bipinnatus* (5)

D *Ageratum houstonianum.* Floss flower (6)

E *Eustoma grandiflorum.* Lisianthus (5)

F *Echinacea purpurea* 'Magnus'.
Purple coneflower (7)

G *Delphinium elatum.* Candle delphinium (3)

H *Zinnia angustifolia,* orange and white (6)

I *Salvia leucantha.* Mexican bush sage (1)

J *Ipomoea tricolor.* Morning glory (1, on trellis)

K *Scabiosa columbaria* 'Butterfly Blue'.
Pincushion flower (3)

L *Francoa ramosa.* Maiden's wreath (3)

M *Achillea* 'Terracotta'. Yarrow (3)

N *Hemerocallis* hybrids. Daylily (1)

O *Thymus pseudolanuginosus.* Woolly thyme 12)

P *Hydrangea macrophylla.* Bigleaf hydrangea (1)

Q *Digitalis purpurea.* Common foxglove (7)

R *Centaurea cineraria.* Dusty miller (3)

S *Lavandula angustifolia.* English lavender (3)

T *Liatrus spicata.* Gayfeather (1)

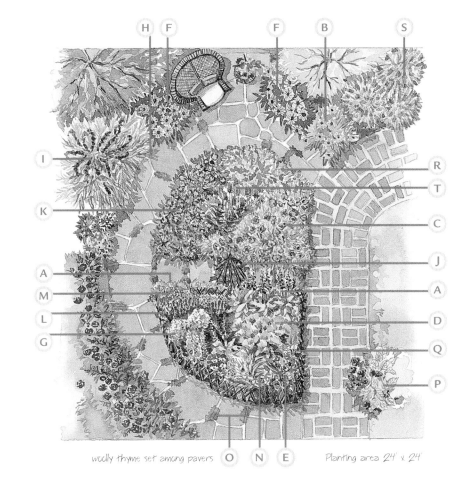

woolly thyme set among pavers   Planting area 24' x 24'

Lavandula angustifolia

plant list

A *Achillea ptarmica* 'The Pearl'. Yarrow (9)

B *Campanula glomerata*, Alba strain. Bellflower (6)

C *Convallaria majalis*. Lily-of-the-valley (12)

D *Delphinium elatum* 'Summer Skies' and 'Galahad'. Candle delphinium (9)

E *Digitalis purpurea*, Excelsior strain. Common foxglove (7)

F *Filipendula rubra* 'Venusta'. Queen of the prairie (5)

G *Gypsophila paniculata* 'Bristol Fairy'. Baby's breath (5)

H *Lavandula angustifolia* 'Hidcote'. English lavender (6)

I *Linum perenne*. Perennial blue flax (14)

J *Monarda didyma* 'Croftway Pink'. Bee balm (4)

K *Nigella damascena* 'Persian Jewels'. Love-in-a-mist (19)

L *Rosa gallica* 'Versicolor' ('Rosa Mundi') (2)

M *Rosa* 'Climbing Cécile Brunner' (2)

N *Viola × wittrockiana*, Imperial Antique Shades strain. Pansy (20)

COTTAGE CORNER Soft, fragrant, and colored in whites, creams, pinks, and blues—this is a cottage garden for fairy tales and romances. Many of the plants are frothy, billowy, and filmy, but the spikes of delphinium, foxglove, and campanula provide sharp vertical punctuation. Late spring and early summer find the garden at the zenith of its bloom. Zones 4–9, 14–16, and 32 suit all the plants listed; the plan will also succeed in Zones 34 and 39 if you substitute deep pink *Rosa* 'William Baffin' for 'Climbing Cécile Brunner' (M in the list at right).

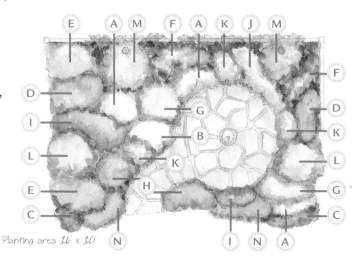

Planting area 16' x 10'

A LESS-THIRSTY COTTAGE GARDEN Even if water is in short supply, a cottage garden isn't out of the question. This garden is built with plants that get by with just moderate moisture during the gowing season. The plants here are suited to Zones 3–10, 14–24, 32–34, and 39. Gardeners in Zones 2, 30, 35–38, 40, and 41 can achieve the same general look by replacing the Oriental fountain grass (J) with tufted fescue *(Festuca amethystina)* and the lavender (L) with blue mist *(Caryopteris × clandonensis)*.

plant list

A *Hibiscus syriacus* 'Blue Bird'. Rose of Sharon (1)

B *Achillea* 'Moonshine'. Yarrow (1)

C *Asclepias tuberosa*. Butterfly weed (5)

D *Scabiosa atropurpurea*. Pincushion flower (5)

E *Coreopsis tinctoria*. Annual coreopsis (3)

F *Echinacea purpurea*. Purple coneflower (3)

G *Verbena × hybrida*. Garden verbena (5)

H *Euphorbia polychroma*. Cushion spurge (5)

I *Agastache foeniculum*. Anise hyssop (2)

J *Pennisetum orientale*. Oriental fountain grass (2)

K *Nepeta grandiflora*. Catmint (3)

L *Lavandula angustifolia*. English lavender (2)

M *Stachys byzantina* 'Silver Carpet'. Lamb's ears (6)

Planting area 11 × 6

COMPLEAT COTTAGE GARDEN Even if you don't have a 19th-century cottage, you can still have the garden that would go with it! The essence of such gardens is informality and apparent lack of plan; they give the impression of growing not by design, but simply according to the gardener's changing whims. Original cottage gardens contained just one representative of many different plants, and cottagers even mixed flowers with vegetables to create plantings that were practical as well as aesthetically pleasing. This contemporary homage to the cottage garden (best suited to Zones 4–7, 14, 34, and 39) excludes the edibles but has all the other traditional characteristics: color, immense variety, and seemingly haphazard design. To adapt the plan to Zones 3, 35–38, 40, and 41, simply replace the lavender (F in the list at right) with blue mist (*Caryopteris* × *clandonensis* 'Dark Knight' or 'Longwood Blue').

plant list

A *Rosa* 'Cornelia' (1)

B *Rosa* 'Ballerina' (1)

C *Rosa* 'Iceberg' (1)

D *Syringa vulgaris* 'President Lincoln'. Common lilac (1)

E *Spiraea japonica* 'Anthony Waterer'. Spirea (2)

F *Lavandula angustifolia.* English lavender (4)

G *Paeonia* 'Festiva Maxima'. Peony (3)

H *Gypsophila paniculata* 'Perfecta'. Baby's breath (3)

I *Foeniculum vulgare* 'Purpurascens'. Bronze fennel (1)

J *Alcea rosea,* Chater's Double strain. Hollyhock (3)

K *Delphinium elatum* 'Summer Skies'. Candle delphinium (7)

L *Lupinus,* Russell hybrids. Russell lupine (3)

M *Achillea filipendulina* 'Coronation Gold'. Fernleaf yarrow (5)

N *Chrysanthemum maximum* 'Alaska'. Shasta daisy (6)

O *Campanula persicifolia* 'Telham Beauty'. Peach-leafed bluebell (5)

P *Aster × frikartii* 'Mönch' (6)

Q *Iris,* tall bearded, light yellow cultivar (7)

R *Geranium × oxonianum* 'Claridge Druce'. Cranesbill (4)

S *Scabiosa caucasica.* Pincushion flower (6)

T *Salvia officinalis* 'Tricolor'. Common sage (4)

U *Heuchera sanguinea.* Coral bells (8)

V *Dianthus plumarius.* Cottage pink (5)

W *Sedum* 'Autumn Joy'. Stonecrop (5)

X *Lychnis coronaria.* Crown-pink (5)

Y *Stachys byzantina* 'Silver Carpet'. Lamb's ears (5)

Z *Aurinia saxatilis.* Basket-of-gold (4)

AA *Lobularia maritima.* Sweet alyssum, set among pavers (12)

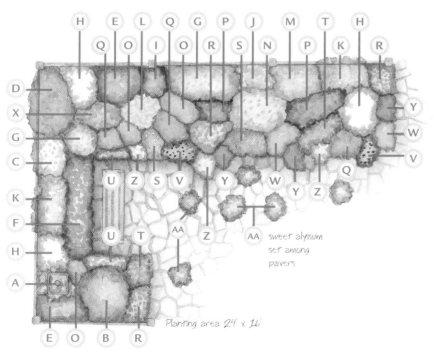

Planting area 24' × 16'

AA sweet alyssum set among pavers

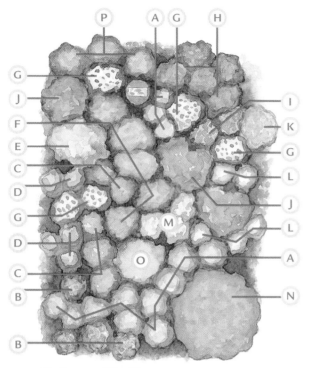

Planting area 22' x 32'

plant list

A *Achillea* 'Heidi'. Yarrow (13)

B *Salvia greggii.* Autumn sage (4)

C *Lavandula stoechas.* Spanish lavender (5)

D *Tulbaghia violacea.* Society garlic (5)

E *Ruta graveolens.* Rue (1)

F *Artemisia* 'Powis Castle' (5)

G *Chrysanthemum parthenium* 'Aureum'. Golden feverfew (5)

H *Cardoon* (5)

I *Salvia darcyi.* Darcy sage (2)

J *Salvia leucantha.* Mexican bush sage (3)

K *Stipa gigantea.* Giant feather grass (1)

L *Nicotiana sylvestris.* Flowering tobacco (5)

M *Verbascum bombyciferum* 'Arctic Summer'. Mullein (3)

N *Teucrium fruticans* 'Azureum'. Bush germander (1)

O *Nassella tenuissima.* Mexican feather grass (1)

P *Salvia canariensis.* Canary Island sage (3)

UNTHIRSTY AND DEER RESISTANT This hillside border mimics nature, with a "river" of 'Powis Castle' artemisia studded with "boulders" of society garlic and Mexican bush sage; a fountain of Mexican feather grass erupts just below. This stunning garden for Zones 14–24 can handle sun, drought, and even stands up to hungry deer.

plant list

A *Miscanthus sinensis*
'Morning Light'. Eulalia, Japanese silver grass (1)

B *Calamagrostis × acutiflora* 'Karl Foerster'.
Feather reed grass (1)

C *Stipa gigantea.* Giant feather grass (2)

D *Molinia caerulea.* Purple moor grass (2)

E *Helictotrichon sempervirens.* Blue oat grass (5)

F *Pennisetum alopecuroides* 'Hameln'.
Fountain grass (5)

G *Festuca glauca* 'Elijah Blue'.
Common blue fescue (8)

H *Perovskia.* Russian sage (1)

I *Rudbeckia fulgida sullivantii* 'Goldsturm' (5)

J *Echinacea purpurea* 'White Swan'. Coneflower (3)

K *Liatris spicata* 'Silvertips'. Gayfeather (3)

L *Achillea filipendulina* 'Coronation Gold'.
Fernleaf yarrow (4)

M *Achillea millefolium,* Galaxy strain.
Common yarrow (5)

N *Achillea* 'Moonshine'. Yarrow (5)

O *Gaillardia × grandiflora* 'Goblin'.
Blanket flower (6)

A BACKYARD PRAIRIE

You don't have to live in the Midwest to enjoy a view of the prairie out your window: this backyard planting evokes the spirit of the plains, of sweeps of tall grass dotted with native daisies. It's less uniform in appearance than a true prairie, though, with a variety of grasses and perennial flowers set out in discrete drifts. Count on these plants for toughness and relatively trouble-free performance in Zones 4–9, 14–17, 32–34. By replacing the giant feather grass (C in the list at left) with purple moor grass (*Molinia caerulea arundinacea* 'Skyracer'), the plan will also succeed in Zones 3, 35, 37, and 39.

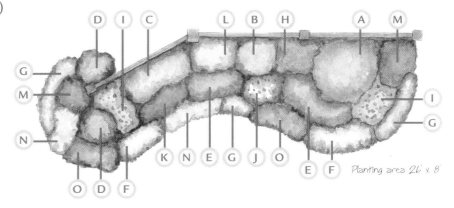

Planting area 26' x 8'

plant list

A *Mahonia japonica* Bealei Group.
 Leatherleaf mahonia (1)

B *Rhododendron*
 'Moonstone' (1)

C *Alchemilla mollis.*
 Lady's-mantle (3)

D *Milium effusum*
 'Aureum'.
 Bowles' golden grass (3)

E *Hosta* 'Gold Edger'.
 Plantain lily (16)

F *Lamium maculatum*
 'White Nancy'. Dead nettle (18)

G × *Heucherella* 'Pink Frost' (5)

H *Athyrium niponicum* 'Pictum'.
 Japanese painted fern (5)

I *Sagina subulata.* Irish moss (about
 sixteen 3-inch squares, set 6 inches apart)

J *Nymphaea,* hardy hybrid. Water lily
 (optional) (1)

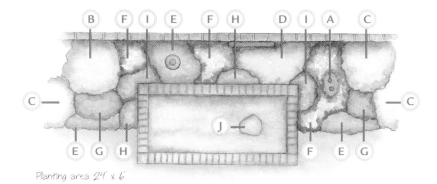

Planting area 24' x 6'

A SHADED POOL Soothing shade and tranquil water are sure to ease stress and restore the spirit. No strident colors assault the eye, demanding attention; instead, chartreuse and silvery leaves offer a counterpoint to basic green, while a smattering of pastel blossoms assort with the foliage in subtly attractive combinations. Bloom is most noticeable (though never overwhelming) in spring and summer. This serenity can be yours if you garden in Zones 4–9, 14–17, 32, and 34.

plant list

A *Iris virginica.* Southern blue flag (3)

B *Iris pseudacorus.* Yellow flag (3)

C *Carex morrowii* 'Variegata'. Variegated Japanese sedge (5)

D *Juncus effusus.* Soft rush (1)

E *Acorus gramineus* 'Variegatus'. Japanese sweet flag (2)

F *Chelone lyonii.* Turtlehead (3)

G *Caltha palustris.* Marsh marigold (2)

H *Aruncus dioicus.* Goat's beard (1)

I *Filipendula ulmaria.* Meadowsweet (1)

J *Eupatorium coelestinum* 'Cori'. Hardy ageratum (4)

K *Astilbe chinensis taquetii* 'Purple Lance'. False spirea (3)

L *Astilbe simplicifolia* 'Sprite'. False spirea (6)

M *Ligularia stenocephala* 'The Rocket' (3)

GONE FISHIN' You'd almost expect to find fish biting in this naturalistic pond. If you don't have a natural pond, you can create your own pool and take the plan from there. Noteworthy is the assortment of foliage types: grasslike in rush and sedge, swordlike in irises and acorus, finely cut and fernlike in goat's beard and astilbe, huge and paddlelike in the ligularia. Flowering runs from spring through early fall, beginning with irises and marsh marigold and finishing with turtlehead, hardy ageratum, and astilbe. Try this plan in Zones 3–7, 15–17, 32, 34, and 36–41.

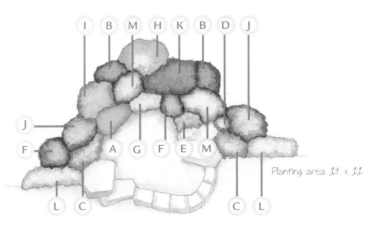

Planting area 14' x 11'

water, captured

tom's notebook

The sound of splashing water draws you to this enchanting garden. Coming down the stairs, you see a pond edged by mossy bricks that look like they've been there for ages. Then you discover the lovely focal point you only heard before—a fountain in the shape of a giant gunnera leaf perched upon a brick wall. Low-profile brick pads seem to float on the pond's surface among water lilies, blue-flowered pickerel weed, and a variegated canna grown as an aquatic.

Although the garden seems cool and shady, it actually receives quite a bit of dappled sunlight, as evidenced by the thriving euphorbia that hugs the fountain and the sun-loving purple wallflowers at the base of the steps. The warm red of a fuchsia and the bright yellow of a variegated loosestrife heat up the scene behind the fountain, and those fiery tones —plus orange—are picked up again in the foreground zinnias.

Tom

1 Leaving open space in the pool allows for a mirror effect

2 The occasional missing brick is replaced by low ground cover

3 A large pot with phormium adds a note of formality

4 Dramatic plants are in scale with the over-sized water feature

AN ALPINE NOOK A gentle, rocky slope is the perfect setting for this group of shrubs and perennials with low water needs. The majority of these plants are particularly suited to low elevations and coastal gardens, such as Zones 9, 15–24, but most of these plants will also do well in Zones 2–8, 10–14, 32–33. Some are California natives; others are Mediterranean in origin. Their foliage textures and flowers will supply interest throughout the year.

plant list

A *Achillea* 'Moonshine'. Yarrow (3)

B *Armeria maritima.* Common thrift (3)

C *Asteriscus maritimus* 'Gold Coin' (3)

D *Cerastium tomentosum.* Snow-in-summer (3)

E *Chamaecyparis obtusa* 'Torulosa'. Hinoki false cypress (1)

F *Dianthus knappii.* Hardy garden pink (3)

G *Eriogonum umbellatum* 'Polyanthum'. Sulfur flower (3)

H *Imperata cylindrica* 'Rubra'. Japanese blood grass (3)

I *Rosmarinus officinalis* 'Collingwood Ingram'. Rosemary (3)

J *Santolina chamaecyparissus.* Lavender cotton (3)

K *Sisyrinchium idahoense bellum.* Blue-eyed grass (3)

L *Nassella tenuissima.* Mexican feather grass (3)

M *Thymus praecox arcticus* 'Reiter's'. Mother-of-thyme (5)

Planting area 16' x 12'

plant list

A *Arabis caucasica* ‘Flore Plena’. Wall rockcress (3)

B *Arctostaphylos uva-ursi* ‘Vancouver Jade’.
   Bearberry (2)

C *Armeria maritima* ‘Rubrifolia’. Common thrift (5)

D *Artemisia schmidtiana* ‘Silver Mound’.
   Angel’s hair (1)

E *Aurinia saxatilis* ‘Sunny Border Apricot’.
   Basket-of-gold (1)

F *Cerastium tomentosum columnae.*
   Snow-in-summer (3)

G *Festuca glauca* ‘Elijah Blue’. Common blue fescue (2)

H *Geranium dalmaticum.* Cranesbill (3)

I *Juniperus squamata* ‘Blue Star.’ Juniper (1)

J *Oenothera macrocarpa.* Ozark sundrops (3)

K *Penstemon pinifolius* ‘Mersea Yellow’.
   Pineleaf penstemon (3)

L *Picea pungens* ‘Montgomery’.
   Dwarf Colorado spruce (1)

M *Scutellaria resinosa.* Prairie skullcap (1)

N *Sedum* ‘Vera Jameson’. Stonecrop (1)

O *Veronica spicata incana.* Silver speedwell (3)

A MINIATURE MOUNTAIN Like picture postcards of nature, rock gardens simulate boulder-strewn mountain slopes or rocky coastal bluffs dotted with small flowering or evergreen plants. True alpine plants grow on high mountain slopes, but many of these plants also prosper at elevations far lower than their native habitats, providing the soil is well drained. And small flowering bulbs, perennials, and dwarf shrubs native to windy and dry-summer areas of Asia, Europe, and other parts of the world also do well in rock gardens, as proved by this planting designed for Zones 33, 35, 41, 43, and 45.

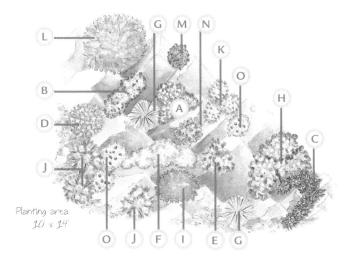

Planting area
10ʹ x 14ʹ

plant list

A *Polypodium scolopendria.* Wart fern (13)

B *Sansevieria trifasciata* 'Black Gold'. Bowstring hemp, snake plant (16)

C *Philodendron subincisum* (3)

D *Dioon mejiae* (1)

E *Rhapis excelsa.* Lady palm (3)

F *Clerodendrum splendens.* Red clerodendrum (3)

G *Neoregelia* 'Compacta' (6)

H *Neoregelia* 'Royal Burgundy' (9)

I *Heterocentron elegans.* Spanish shawl (23)

J *Peperomia obtusifolia* 'Variegata' (9)

K *Anthurium* 'Ruffles'. Spathe flower (1)

FUTURE LOOK A house style this distinctive deserves a garden to match. That's certainly the case here, where the sculptural plantings echo the sculptural look of the house. This tropical garden features plants that are used are generally grown as houseplants in other areas of the country, but they thrive in the outdoors in Zones 23–25 and H2.

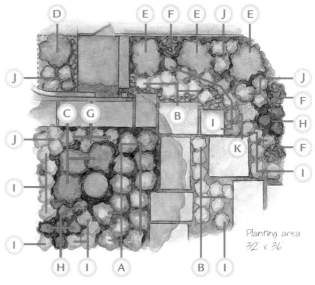

Planting area
32 x 36

SUCCULENT DISPLAY Lush, yet drought tolerant, this small garden is filled with some of the many succulents that thrive in well-drained soils. The repetition of rosette-forming succulents unifies the composition. The silver and gray foliage of the aeoniums and *Aloe striata* enlivens the green palette, while brilliant red *Crassula falcata* and nearly black *Aeonium arboreum* 'Zwartkop' provide dramatic accents. Though the plants won't take cold winters, they do well in Zones 17 and 21–24.

plant list

A *Aeonium arboreum* 'Zwartkop'. Black aenonium (3)

B *Aeonium urbicum* (3)

C *Aeonium decorum* (3)

D *Aloe aristata* (3)

E *Aloe striata*. Coral aloe (1)

F *Cotyledon undulata* (1)

G *Crassula falcata* (3)

H *Dudleya brittonii* (1)

I *Echeveria agavoides* (3)

J *Echeveria × imbricata*. Hen and chicks (5)

K *Haworthia fasciata*. Zebra haworthia (3)

L *Sedum album*. Stonecrop (3)

M *Sedum × rubrotinctum*. Pork and beans (3)

N *Sedum spathulifolium* 'Purpureum'. Stonecrop (5)

O *Senecio mandraliscae* (1)

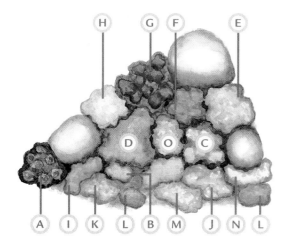

Planting area 6' x 8'

This is a true flower-lover's garden, with its ebullient good looks enlivening the landscape and plenty of blooms to pick and bring indoors. Creating this carefree effect began with choosing plants that suit the climate, then arranging them to complement and contrast with each other. And everything was positioned with ease of maintenance in mind.

flower gardens

For many people, the words "flower" and "garden" are synonymous. These plans are for just those gardeners. Fortunately, many favorite flowers are also flexible in their climate requirements, so these eight gardens do well in many different areas.

Looking through the plans will show there's something to suit almost everyone. There's a garden filled with easy-to-grow annuals that are ideal for a first-time gardener. There are gardens designed to ensure perennial flower color from spring through fall. For the rose lover, several plans will fill a large space with these favorites, and others will work well even if there is very little room. And for even more flower garden ideas, look at the cottage garden plans on pages 128 to 133 and at the ideas for color gardens on pages 168 to 181.

One of the best reasons to grow flowers, of course, is to have them for bouquets. That's where flower gardens shine. The more flowers you cut, the harder your plant will work to produce even more flowers. Follow this rule, and you can have your flowers and cut them, too.

These tough perennial beauties bloom nearly nonstop from spring into fall, brightening a tired corner of this garden. Including foliage plants adds texture and structure to the space.

plant list

A *Echinacea purpurea.* Purple coneflower (2)

B *Cosmos bipinnatus,* Sonata strain (5)

C *Zinnia elegans* (7)

D *Senecio cineraria.* Dusty miller (3)

E *Lobularia maritima.* Sweet alyssum (4)

F *Cerastium tomentosum.* Snow-in-summer (2)

G *Tagetes erecta.* African marigold (5)

H *Nassella tenuissima.* Mexican feather grass (3)

I *Petunia* × *hybrida* (3)

FIRST-TIME FLOWER GARDEN Designed for a beginning gardener, this easy-to-grow planting provides color, and plenty of flowers for bouquets, all summer long. The plants can be grown almost anywhere as annuals and offer almost-instant flowering gratification. To keep the bloom going, cut off all the flowers (not buds) when you plant, and keep cutting and deadheading throughout the season.

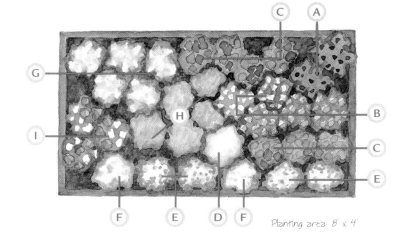

Planting area: 8' x 4'

plant list

A *Kniphofia*, yellow cultivar.
Red-hot poker (1)

B *Baptisia australis.*
Blue false indigo (1)

C *Paeonia* 'Festiva Maxima'.
Peony (2)

D *Centranthus ruber* 'Albus'.
Jupiter's beard (4)

E *Penstemon barbatus*
'Pink Beauty'. Scarlet bugler (3)

F *Aster × frikartii* 'Mönch' (4)

G *Chrysanthemum coccineum.*
Pyrethrum, painted daisy (3)

H *Iris*, Siberian, 'Caesar's Brother' (1)

I *Hemerocallis*, cream cultivar. Daylily (2)

J *Hemerocallis* 'Stella de Oro'. Daylily (4)

K *Gaura lindheimeri* 'Siskiyou Pink' (1)

L *Geranium* 'Johnson's Blue'. Cranesbill (4)

M *Papaver orientale*, pink cultivar. Oriental poppy (1)

N *Geum chiloense* 'Lady Stratheden' (2)

O *Heuchera micrantha* 'Palace Purple'. Coral bells (6)

P *Iberis sempervirens* 'Snowflake'. Evergreen candytuft (2)

Q *Campanula portenschlagiana.* Dalmatian bellflower (2)

R *Aurinia saxatilis.* Basket-of-gold (3)

SPRING SYMPHONY As winter's drear slowly gives way to brighter days, nothing is more heartening than flowers. The cheerful assortment of perennials shown here captures all the color and bounty of spring in one compact planting. You'll have the best results with this plan in climates offering some winter chill (Zones 3–9, 14–16, 33, and 34). You can also employ it in Zones 2, 35–41 if you make a few substitutions: in place of red-hot poker (A in the list at left), use three plants of foxtail lily *(Eremurus,* Shelford hybrids); for gaura (K), substitute three *Penstemon digitalis* 'Husker Red', and for *Geranium* 'Johnson's Blue' (L), use meadow cranesbill *(G. pratense).*

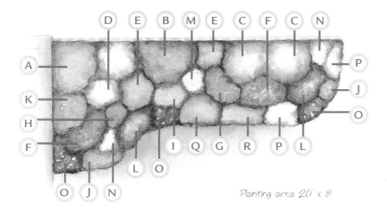

Planting area 20' × 8'

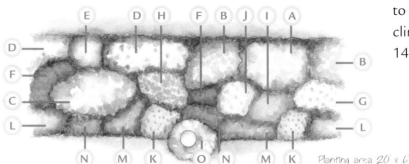

plant list

A *Dictamnus albus* 'Albiflorus'. Gas plant (2)

B *Achillea millefolium,* Summer Pastels strain. Common yarrow (3+)

C *Achillea* 'Moonshine'. Yarrow (4)

D *Echinacea purpurea* 'White Swan'. Coneflower (7+)

E *Artemisia lactiflora.* White mugwort (1)

F *Liatris spicata* 'Kobold'. Gayfeather (4)

G *Chrysanthemum maximum* 'Aglaia'. Shasta daisy (5+)

H *Limonium platyphyllum.* Sea lavender (3)

I *Hemerocallis,* cream cultivar. Daylily (2)

J *Coreopsis verticillata* 'Moonbeam' (1)

K *Coreopsis auriculata* 'Nana' (3)

L *Veronica* 'Goodness Grows'. Speedwell (4+)

M *Verbena* 'Homestead Purple' (4)

N *Potentilla nepalensis* 'Miss Willmott'. Cinquefoil (4)

O *Cerastium tomentosum.* Snow-in-summer (7)

SUMMER SPLENDOR Spring may usher in the flowering year, but summer's show is no less dazzling. In fact, many summer-blooming perennials mount a longer lasting display than spring bloomers do, staying showy throughout the summer and even into autumn. In keeping with the season's temperatures, many of these perennials offer distinctly warm colors. In the plan illustrated here, summery hues of yellow and rosy red are balanced with plenty of white and blue, cool shades that offer welcome (if only psychological!) relief on scorching days. These plants are suited to a wide range of climates: Zones 2–9, 14–17, 32–43.

Planting area 20' x 6'

HARVEST BOUNTY Autumn clearly signals the close of the gardening year—but it's a terrific last act, brimming with color. Most of the flowering plants in this plan hold their fire through spring and summer, bursting into bloom only when the shorter, crisper days of fall arrive. Try this plan as an autumn pick-me-up in Zones 3–21, 31–35, 37, 39. To enjoy it in Zones 2, 36, 38, 40, and 41 as well, substitute purple moor grass *(Molinia caerulea)* for the fountain grass (B in the list below).

Planting area 20 × 7

plant list

A *Calamagrostis × acutiflora* 'Karl Foerster'. Feather reed grass (3)

B *Pennisetum alopecuroides.* Fountain grass (2)

C *Helictotrichon sempervirens.* Blue oat grass (2)

D *Boltonia asteroides* 'Snowbank' (4)

E *Heliopsis helianthoides* 'Golden Plume'. Ox-eye sunflower (4)

F *Solidago* 'Goldenmosa'. Goldenrod (3)

G *Aster novi-belgii* 'Audrey'. New York aster (2)

H *Aster novi-belgii* 'Marie Ballard'. New York aster (2)

I *Helenium autumnale* 'Brilliant'. Sneezeweed (2)

J *Hemerocallis* 'Parian China'. Daylily (2)

K *Sedum* 'Autumn Joy'. Stonecrop (5)

L *Chrysanthemum pacificum.* Gold and silver chrysanthemum (2)

M *Chrysanthemum arcticum.* Arctic chrysanthemum (3)

N *Chrysanthemum × grandiflorum,* cream or light yellow cushion type. Florists' chrysanthemum (7)

149

roses and perennials | creating a tapestry

Creating a colorful garden that can also stand up to summer heat and dry conditions calls for rugged ornamentals, such as the heat-loving plants that fill this garden. Brightly colored masses of sturdy daylilies, carpeting roses, small shrubs, and ornamental grasses repeated throughout the entire bed create year-round texture and color, while stands of gray 'Powis Castle' artemisia separate the blocks of color into islands. The undulating stone wall that surrounds the property sets off this colorful border magnificently.

Low-growing plantings blur the boundary between the patio and the garden.

Planting beds are bermed, to allow for good drainage, and pathways between these plantings allow easy access to all parts of the bed.

plant list

A *Stachys byzantina* 'Primrose Heron'. Lamb's ears

B *Agapanthus* 'Mood Indigo'. Lily-of-the-Nile

C *Rosa* 'Flower Carpet', pink

D *Dierama robustum.* Fairy wand

E *Lavandula* 'Goodwin Creek Grey'. Lavender

F *Berberis thunbergii* 'Rose Glow'. Japanese berberry

G *Origanum* 'Norton Gold'. Oregano

H *Geranium* × *cantabrigiense.* Cranesbill

I *Nepeta* × *faasenii* 'Blue Wonder'. Catmint

J *Artemisia* 'Powis Castle'

ROSES IN THE GRAND MANNER If rosemania strikes and you have the space to indulge it to the full, succumb to your desires with this formal design. It accommodates 51 plants, ranging from climbers to miniatures. In maintenance terms, Zones 4–9, 12–24, 30, 32 are best for this planting, but it will also work in Zones 11, 33, 34, and 39 with winter protection for the roses (you need to overwinter the potted lily turf in a frost-sheltered spot in Zones 34 and 39).

Planting area 34' × 28'

plant list

A *Rosa* 'New Dawn' (1)

B *Rosa* 'Abraham Darby' (1)

C *Rosa* 'Graham Thomas' (1)

D *Rosa* 'The Fairy', as standard (2)

E *Rosa,* hybrid tea (assorted) (26)

F *Rosa,* floribunda cultivar (2)

G *Rosa,* miniature (assorted) (18)

H *Lavandula × intermedia* 'Grosso'. Lavandin (6)

I *Lavandula angustifolia* 'Hidcote'. English lavender (8)

J *Artemisia stelleriana* 'Silver Brocade'. Beach wormwood (14)

K *Liriope muscari* 'Majestic'. Big blue lily turf (in urn) (1)

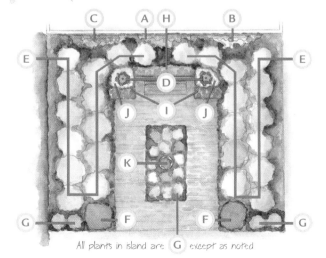

All plants in island are (G) except as noted

plant list

A *Rosa* 'Climbing Iceberg' (1)

B *Rosa* 'Altissimo' (1)

C *Rosa* 'Queen Elizabeth' (1)

D *Rosa* 'Peace' (1)

E *Rosa* 'Fragrant Cloud' (1)

F *Rosa* 'Mister Lincoln' (1)

G *Rosa* 'Double Delight' (1)

H *Rosa* 'Pascali' (1)

I *Rosa* 'Perfume Delight' (1)

J *Rosa* 'Amber Queen' (1)

K *Rosa* 'Europeana' (1)

L *Rosa* 'Angel Face' (1)

M *Lavandula angustifolia* 'Munstead'. English lavender (5)

N *Geranium himalayense* 'Plenum' (2)

O *Geranium cinereum* 'Ballerina'. Cranesbill (4)

P *Potentilla nepalensis* 'Miss Willmott'. Cinquefoil (4)

Q *Dianthus plumarius.* Cottage pink (9)

R *Stachys byzantina.* Lamb's ears (9)

S *Cerastium tomentosum.* Snow-in-summer (6)

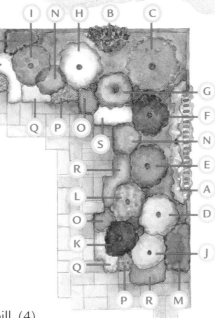

Planting area 16' x 21'

A ROSY CORNER So many choices, so little space! For many gardeners, that's the annual lament at bare-root planting time, when nurseries are flooded with roses of all sorts, from brand-new hybrid teas to old-fashioned heritage types. If you have only a modest plot available, make the most of it with this design. Including just 12 different roses, it nonetheless offers the full spectrum of colors in varieties of proven performance and popularity. An assortment of perennials fronts the bed, serving as a colorful, informal transition between the rather stiff rose bushes and the surrounding paving. Zones 4–9, 12–24, and 32 are best for this plan, but you can also use it in Zones 33, 34, and 39 if you give the roses winter protection.

ROSES FROM THE PAST The roses of yesterday are not outmoded or obsolete. Quite to the contrary, they're being rediscovered, retrieved, and cherished by thousands of gardeners enchanted by the styles and histories of old or "heritage" roses. Unlike most modern hybrid teas, grandifloras, and floribundas, many heritage sorts are informal to lax shrubs that should not be planted in stiff, precisely spaced ranks. Give them room to mound, sprawl, or droop, then enjoy the resulting floral resplendence. This plan features eight old rose types—gallica, damask, alba, moss, China, tea, Noisette, and polyantha—in colors ranging from white and soft yellow to pink shades and deep red. Accompanying the roses are assorted perennials, many of them also suitably antique. Zones 4–9, 14–24 yield the best results; with winter protection of the climbers, Zone 32 is also possible.

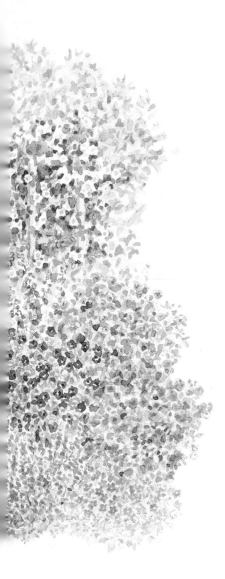

plant list

A *Rosa* 'Awakening' (1)

B *Rosa* 'Sombreuil' (1)

C *Rosa* 'Alister Stella Gray' (1)

D *Rosa* 'Alba Maxima' (1)

E *Rosa* 'Great Maiden's Blush' (1)

F *Rosa* 'Mme. Lambard'
('Mme. Lombard') (1)

G *Rosa* 'Duchesse de Brabant' (1)

H *Rosa* 'Marie Louise' (1)

I *Rosa* 'Paul Ricault' (1)

J *Rosa* 'Alfred de Dalmas' (1)

K *Rosa* 'Empress Josephine' (1)

L *Rosa* 'Perle d'Or' (1)

M *Rosa* 'Hermosa' (1)

N *Rosa* 'Comte de Chambord' (1)

O *Rosa* 'Superb Tuscan'
('Tuscany Superb') (1)

P *Rosa* 'Grüss an Aachen' (1)

Q *Rosa* 'Pink Grüss an Aachen' (1)

R *Ilex cornuta* 'Dazzler'. Chinese holly (6+)

S *Juniperus chinensis* 'Hetz's Columnaris'.
Chinese juniper (5)

T *Digitalis purpurea*. Common foxglove (10)

U *Lavandula × intermedia* 'Provence'.
Lavandin (6)

V *Centranthus ruber* 'Albus'. Jupiter's beard (7)

W *Geranium pratense*. Meadow cranesbill (4)

X *Geranium sanguineum*. Bloody cranesbill (4)

Y *Nepeta × faassenii*. Catmint (7)

Z *Dianthus plumarius*. Cottage pink (8)

AA *Iberis sempervirens* 'Snowflake'.
Evergreen candytuft (4)

BB *Aurinia saxatilis* 'Citrina' ('Lutea').
Basket-of-gold (5)

CC *Stachys byzantina* 'Silver Carpet'.
Lamb's ears (7)

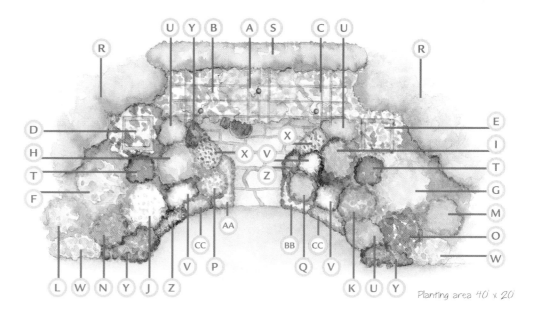

Planting area 40' x 20'

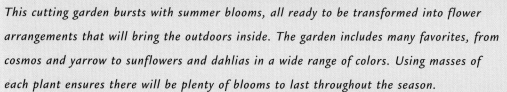

This cutting garden bursts with summer blooms, all ready to be transformed into flower arrangements that will bring the outdoors inside. The garden includes many favorites, from cosmos and yarrow to sunflowers and dahlias in a wide range of colors. Using masses of each plant ensures there will be plenty of blooms to last throughout the season.

plantings plus

A beautiful garden is always a gardener's goal. Sometimes, though, mere loveliness is not enough. In those cases, the garden also needs to serve a specific purpose or meet a specific need. It might be a cutting garden, designed to produce armloads of flowers throughout the year. It might be a place to grow herbs or vegetables. It might even be a space designed to attract birds, butterflies, and other wild creatures.

The ten gardens that follow are just such designs. Four cutting garden plans will please those who like to take the garden indoors throughout most, if not all, of the year. The four plans for kitchen and herb gardens will delight cooks; one of these plans even allows you to mix your edibles with flowers. And for backyard naturalists, we've devised gardens that will be sure to entice birds and buttterflies to make themselves at home.

A formal garden design is both a traditional and an effective choice for an herb garden. Geometric paths allow easy access; the plants add softness to a sometimes stark look.

Planting area 14 x 6

⭐ **SPRINGTIME FLOWER FACTORY** This planting looks lush, perhaps even a bit wild—but its exuberance disguises a hard-working and efficient setup. Plants A through G are perennials and can be expected to last for several to many years in Zones 4–10, 14–20, 32 41. Where winters are nearly frost-free, choose a peony (A) with a Japanese flower form: it needs the least winter chill. The tulips (H) may need annual replacing in warmer-winter regions. The anemones (I) must be dug and stored over winter where lows regularly dip below 0°F/18°C; the freesias (J) need digging and storage below 20°F/–7°C.

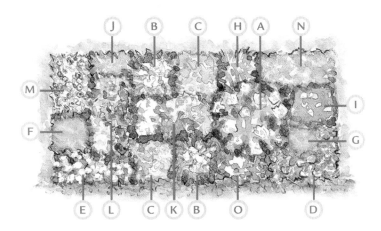

plant list

A *Paeonia,* herbaceous hybrid (e.g. 'Festiva Maxima'). Peony (1)

B *Iris,* tall bearded cultivar (e.g. 'Silverado', 'Beverly Sills') (6)

C *Aquelegia,* McKana, Giants strain. Columbine (8)

D *Dianthus caryophyllus.* Carnation (6)

E *Iberis sempervirens.* Evergreen candytuft (4)

F *Primula,* Polyanthus Group. Polyanthus primrose (4)

G *Narcissus,* trumpet or large-cupped cultivar (e.g. 'Mount Hood', 'Ice Follies'). Daffodil (5)

H *Tulipa,* mixed Single Late types. Tulip (8)

I *Anemone coronaria.* Poppy-flowered anemone (9)

J *Freesia,* Tecolote hybrid (6)

K *Consolida ajacis,* Steeplechase strain. Larkspur (5)

L *Antirrhinum majus,* Rocket strain. Snapdragon (8)

M *Centaurea cyanus,* Polka Dot strain. Cornflower, bachelor's button (8)

N *Viola × wittrockiana.* Pansy (6)

O *Viola cornuta.* Viola (4)

SUMMER FLOWER FACTORY This 6- by 16-foot cutting garden has been designed for pure efficiency. Over half the plants are brilliant annuals, suitable for all zones, and the other plants will flourish in Zones 1–9, 14–21, 31–41, though you will need to grow Transvaal daisy (E) as an annual where winter lows dip to 15°F/9°C, and you may need to substitute *P. digitalis* for the border penstemon (A) and *Chrysanthemum zawadskii* 'Clara Curtis' for *Coreopsis rosea* (G) in cold-winter climates.

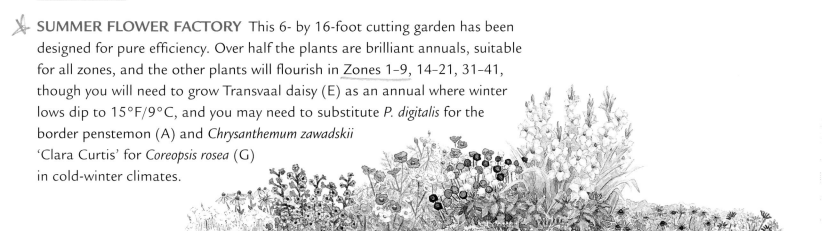

Planting area 16' x 6'

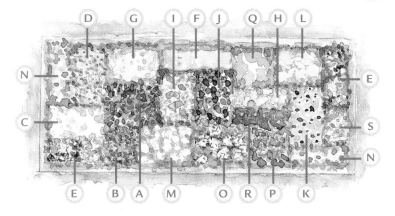

plant list

A *Penstemon* 'Garnet' or *P. digitalis.* Border penstemon or beard tongue (2)

B *Liatris spicata* 'Kobold'. Gayfeather (3)

C *Chrysanthemum maximum* 'Esther Read'. Shasta daisy (4)

D *Echinacea purpurea* 'Bravado'. Purple coneflower (2)

E *Gerbera jamesonii.* Transvaal daisy (6)

F *Veronica spicata* 'Icicle'. Speedwell (3)

G *Coreopsis rosea* or *Chrysanthemum zawadskii* 'Clara Curtis'. Coreopsis or chrysanthemum (4)

H *Gladiolus,* Grandiflora hybrid, light yellow cultivar, summer-flowering or winter hardy type (8)

I *Cosmos bipinnatus,* Versailles strain (6)

J *Scabiosa atropurpurea,* Double Mixed strain. Pincushion flower (8)

K *Rudbeckia hirta* 'Marmalade'. Gloriosa daisy (6)

L *Tagetes erecta,* Perfection strain. African marigold (6)

M *Tagetes erecta,* Sweet Cream strain. African marigold (6)

N *Tagetes patula.* French marigold (10)

O *Zinnia elegans* 'Candy Stripe' (8)

P *Limonium sinuatum.* Statice (6)

Q *Nicotiana alata,* Nicki strain. Flowering tobacco (6)

R *Perilla frutescens.* Shiso (3)

S *Gypsophila paniculata.* Baby's breath (3)

🌾 **FLOWERS FOR FALL** Warm blossom colors and the tawny seed heads of grasses give this planting an unmistakable harvest-time aura: the flowers just beg to be cut and arranged in centerpieces with pumpkins, pomegranates, and other autumn bounty. This planting is largely permanent; only the final four plants need annual removal and replacement. And all the perennials adapt to a wide range of climates, thriving in Zones 2–10, 14–23, and 31–41.

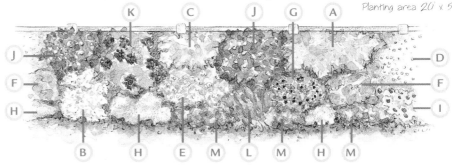

Planting area 20' x 5'

plant list

A *Calamagrostis × acutiflora* 'Karl Foerster'. Feather reed grass (2)

B *Panicum virgatum* 'Heavy Metal'. Switch grass (1)

C *Solidago* 'Goldenmosa'. Goldenrod (2)

D *Aster novi-belgii* 'Marie Ballard'. New York aster (3)

E *Aster amellus*. Italian aster (4)

F *Sedum* 'Autumn Joy'. Stonecrop (3)

G *Helenium* 'Crimson Beauty'. Sneezeweed (2)

H *Chrysanthemum × grandiflorum*, cream or light yellow cushion type. Florists' chrysanthemum (7)

I *Gaillardia × grandiflora* 'Goblin Yellow'. Blanket flower (3)

J *Tithonia rotundifolia*. Mexican sunflower (6)

K *Helianthus annuus* 'Prado Red'. Common sunflower (4)

L *Celosia* 'Apricot Brandy'. Plume cockscomb (5)

M *Tagetes patula*. French marigold (12)

Planting area 25' x 8'

WINTER COLOR Only fortunate gardeners in the West and parts of the South and Southeast can grow a cutting garden for winter arrangements. The garden shown here, hardy to about 0°F/–18°C, is suited to the cooler parts of winter-bloom territory, where cool days and frosty nights are the norm. The alternate plant assortment is almost as hardy, but thrives where winter days are warm and frost is light or absent.

plants for cooler climates

A *Camellia japonica* 'Kramer's Supreme' (1)

B *Corylus avellana* 'Contorta'. Harry Lauder's walking stick (1)

C *Chaenomeles* 'Jet Trail'. Flowering quince (1)

D *Viburnum opulus* 'Compactum'. European cranberry bush (1)

E *Erica carnea* 'Vivellii'. Heath (2)

F *Erica carnea* 'Winter Beauty'. Heath (4)

G *Helleborus orientalis.* Lenten rose (6)

H *Bergenia crassifolia.* Winter-blooming bergenia (3)

I *Primula*, Polyanthus Group. Polyanthus primrose (10)

J *Viola odorata.* Sweet violet (8)

plants for warmer climates

A *Camellia japonica* 'Debutante' (1)

B *Viburnum tinus* 'Spring Bouquet'. Laurustinus (1)

C *Chaenomeles* 'Texas Scarlet'. Flowering quince (1)

D *Nandina domestica* 'Gulf Stream'. Heavenly bamboo (3)

E *Papaver nudicaule.* Iceland poppy (10)

F *Helleborus orientalis.* Lenten rose (8)

G *Rhododendron (azalea),* white-flowered cultivar (e.g. 'Everest', 'Glacier', 'Madonna') (2)

H *Euphorbia × martinii* (5)

I *Calendula officinalis,* cream-colored cultivar (10)

J *Viola × wittrockiana.* Pansy (18)

plant list

A *Thymus vulgaris* 'Italian Oregano Thyme'. Common thyme (6)

B *Thymus vulgaris.* English thyme (4)

C *Thymus × citriodorus.* Lemon thyme (1)

D *Salvia offiicinalis.* Common sage (3)

E *Salvia officinalis* 'Berggarten'. Common sage (2)

F *Cordiothymus capitatus.* Conehead thyme (1)

G *Petroselinum crispum.* Flat-leafed Italian parsley (1)

H *Origanum vulgare hirtum.* Greek oregano (4)

FAVORITE HERBS Mediterranean herbs are some of the most rewarding plants you can grow. And the plants offer a bonus: their leaves flavor everything from meats, soups, and stews to pizza and spaghetti. This garden contains old favorites—parsley, sage, and thyme—as well as some newer introductions, such as conehead thyme, and Italian oregano thyme. The thymes and sages are perennial in Zones 2–24, 30–33, 35–37, 39, and 41; grow the parsley, oregano, and conehead thyme as annuals in the colder zones.

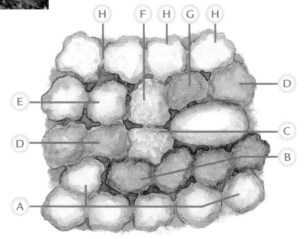

Planting area: 10' × 10'

KITCHEN HERB GARDEN When a modest cornucopia of culinary herbs grows just a few steps away from the kitchen, it's a simple matter to pop outside and snip a few sprigs to add to the dishes simmering indoors. In this plan, two favorites get special planting treatment. Spearmint is confined to a large container to keep its invasive tendencies in check. The bay tree, too, is displayed in its own terracotta pot, since it's suited to year-round outdoor culture only in Zones 5–9, 14–24; in the other regions to which this scheme is adapted (Zones 4, 10, 11, 30–32), it must overwinter in a frost-free shelter. Gardeners in Zone 33 can also use this plan if they choose the rosemary cultivar 'Arp' for (I) in the list to the left. Sweet marjoram (G) will be an annual in Zones 32 and 33; sweet basil (B) is an annual in all zones.

plant list

A *Petroselinum crispum.* Parsley (2)

B *Ocimum basilicum.* Sweet basil (6)

C *Allium schoenoprasum.* Chives (8)

D *Salvia officinalis.* Common sage (2)

E *Origanum vulgare.* Oregano (2)

F *Artemisia dracunculus.* French tarragon (2)

G *Origanum majorana.* Sweet marjoram (1)

H *Satureja montana.* Winter savory (2)

I *Rosmarinus officinalis.* Rosemary (1)

J *Thymus vulgaris.* Common thyme (1)

K *Thymus* × *citriodorus* 'Aureus'. Lemon thyme (1)

L *Mentha spicata.* Spearmint (2)

M *Laurus nobilis.* Sweet bay (1)

Planting area 11 × 6

plant list

A *Capsicum annuum* 'Black Pearl'. Ornamental pepper (2)

B *Ocimum basilicum* 'Mrs. Burns'. Lemon basil (2)

C *Ocimum basilicum* 'Dark Opal'. Basil (3)

D *Salvia longispicata × farinacea* 'Mystic Spires Blue'. Sage (5)

E *Carex dipsacea.* Green sedge (2)

F *Ocimum basilicum* 'Siam Queen'. Thai basil (2)

G *Ocimum basilicum* 'Genovese'. Basil (3)

H *Cuphea llavea* 'Flamenco Rumba'. Bat-faced cuphea (2)

I *Verbena peruviana* hybrid, red (1)

J 'Cayenne' pepper (1)

K 'Listada de Gandia' Italian eggplant (5)

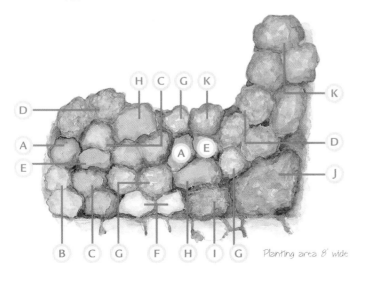

Planting area 8' wide

A COLORFUL MIX Who says vegetable gardens have to be boring? In this 8-foot-wide planting, designed for Zones 11–13, 21–31, brightly colored flowers and edibles are mixed for a striking effect. Lime green and purple basils determine the color scheme, but there are also a red-flowered cuphea (grown as an annual in colder zones), blue-flowered salvias, and a bright red edible pepper, along with splashes of purple courtesy of the eggplant and an ornamental pepper.

plant list

A Apple, dwarfed cultivar (2)

B Asparagus (4)

C Blueberry (2)

D *Calendula officinalis* (8)

E *Allium schoenoprasum.* Chives (6)

F *Monarda didyma* 'Cambridge Scarlet'. Bee balm (2)

G Sweet pepper (5)

H Rhubarb (2)

I *Origanum vulgare.* Oregano (2)

J *Salvia officinalis* 'Icterina'. Common sage (1)

K *Salvia officinalis* 'Purpurascens'. Common sage (1)

L *Salvia officinalis* 'Tricolor'. Common sage (1)

M *Ocimum basilicum* 'Dark Opal'. Sweet basil (6)

N *Thymus × citriodorus* 'Aureus'. Lemon thyme (4)

O *Tropaeolum majus.* Garden nasturtium (4)

MIXED KITCHEN GARDEN Here's a garden of edibles covering a wide culinary spectrum, from fruits to vegetables to savory herbs. The focal point of the design is the living fence of espaliered dwarf apple trees. The nasturtiums, basil, sweet peppers, and calendula are annuals and must be planted anew each year; the remaining fruits and vegetables are perennials or shrubs that need only some annual maintenance or cleanup. Zones 4–6, 17, 32, 34–41 are favorable regions for this planting; to adapt it to Zones 14–16, 30, 31, and 33, replace the blueberry (C in the list at left) with genetic dwarf peach 'Bonanza II'. In Zones 15–17, select an apple cultivar that needs little winter chill.

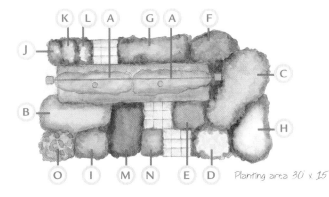

Planting area 30' × 15'

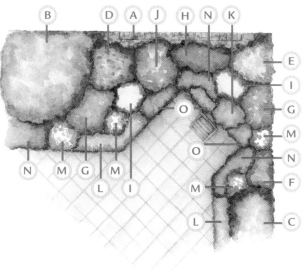

Planting area 18' x 13'

HUMMINGBIRD CORNER

This colorful garden nook offers long-lasting floral bounty: a feast for the gardener's eyes, a literal banquet for humming-birds. The blossoms feature the birds' favorite vivid reds and blues. The tantalizing tableau lures hummers over a prolonged period, beginning in mid- or late spring and continuing through summer (and even into fall, in mild-winter areas). The plants listed here will thrive over much of good hummingbird territory: Zones 2–9, 14–17, 32–41. Note that the three annuals—flowering tobacco, scarlet sage, and petunia—will require replanting each year.

plant list

A *Lonicera periclymenum* 'Serotina'. Woodbine (1)

B *Weigela* 'Bristol Ruby' (1)

C *Weigela* 'Minuet' (1)

D *Monarda didyma* 'Jacob Cline'. Bee balm (6)

E *Alcea rosea*. Hollyhock (7)

F *Digitalis* × *mertonensis*. Foxglove (4)

G *Agastache foeniculum*. Anise hyssop (9)

H *Penstemon barbatus* 'Prairie Fire'. Scarlet bugler (4)

I *Asclepias tuberosa*, yellow cultivar. Butterfly weed (3)

J *Salvia* × *sylvestris* 'Blue Hill'. Sage (6)

K *Lychnis chalcedonica*. Maltese cross (4)

L *Heuchera sanguinea*. Coral bells (9+)

M *Nicotiana alata*, Nicki strain, mixed colors. Flowering tobacco (12)

N *Salvia splendens*, dwarf red strain. Scarlet sage (16)

O *Petunia* × *hybrida*, blue or purple (8)

WESTERN BIRDSCAPE This design is suited to mild-winter Zones 8, 9, 12–24, offering berries, seeds, and shelter. The irresistible lure—as legions of gardeners have come to know—is the yearly crop of firethorn berries, but the garden's feathered patrons will also feast on the fruits of lantana, heavenly bamboo, cotoneaster, and elaeagnus. Seed-eaters will appreciate the bounty of coreopsis, blanket flower, rudbeckia, and fountain grass. The shrubs all afford ample shelter, with the firethorn's forbidding spines providing some protection as well.

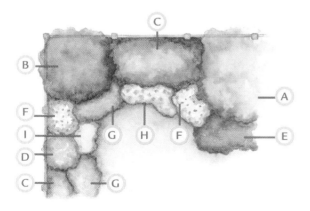

Planting area 25' x 18'

plant list

A *Elaeagnus × ebbingei* (1)

B *Pyracantha coccinea* 'Kasan'. Firethorn (1)

C *Lantana* 'Radiation' (3+)

D *Nandina domestica.* Heavenly bamboo (2)

E *Cotoneaster salicifolius* 'Emerald Carpet'. Willowleaf cotoneaster (2+)

F *Rudbeckia fulgida sullivantii* 'Goldsturm' (11)

G *Pennisetum setaceum.* Fountain grass (6)

H *Gaillardia × grandiflora.* Blanket flower (5)

I *Coreopsis grandiflora* 'Sunburst' (4)

Sometimes a single color makes the most impact. In this border, created to serve as a backdrop for an impressive stone wall and bench, the yellow of the daylilies and black-eyed Susans truly pops when paired with the softer grays and muted greens of the dusty miller and rosemary.

color gardens

Color plays a big role in any garden, but one way to really play it up is to create a color garden. Color gardens are more than just collections of flowering plants. By deliberately choosing plants in either complementary or contrasting colors of both flowers and foliage, a specific look or mood can be created.

Want something cool and refreshing in a dry, hot climate? Consider a garden filled with soft greens and white. Looking for something a little more sophisticated? Change the foliage to white and silver. Trying to capture the sunlight? Plant annuals and perennials featuring yellow-colored blooms. Want to show off a southwestern-style home? Turn to a mix of orange and red to spice up the space around it and create an authentic feel. Or do you like the unexpected? Pair colors like dark purple heliotrope with bright orange kniphofia, or place a lime-green accent plant amid a staid border of dark greens and reds.

The garden plans shown here suggest how you can use various colors in the garden to create just the mood you want.

Though purple and white are the dominant colors in this border, the occasional splashes of pink and orange add contrast without detracting from the overall effect.

plant list

A *Chrysanthemum paludosum* (2)

B *Loropetalum chinense* (2)

C *Sutera cordata.* Bacopa (3)

D *Soleirolia soleirolii.*
Baby's tears (3)

E *Narcissus* 'Thalia'. Daffodil (6)

F *Primula obconica.* Primrose (11)

G *Cyclamen persicum.*
Florists' cyclamen (3)

H *Ophiopogon japonicus* 'Silver
Dragon'. Mondo grass (1)

SNOW WHITE Mild-climate gardeners needn't pine for snow in winter. It's easy to create the look of a light dusting of snow—all frosty and cool—with an all-white planting. Designed for a long season of bloom in Zones 14–24, the planting shown here covers a two-tiered rock retaining wall. Primroses and cyclamen tucked among the stones bloom from fall through spring. Perennial bacopa provides lacy white flowers around them. Come late winter, white narcissus pop up, and by spring the garden is in full color.

Planting area 12' x 7'

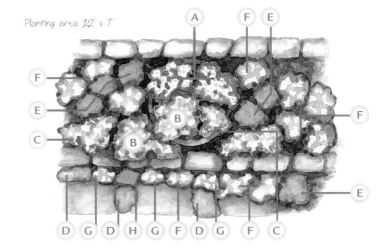

plant list

A *Paeonia,* white cultivar. Peony (1)

B *Dictamnus albus* 'Albiflorus'. Gas plant (3)

C *Baptisia australis.* Blue false indigo (3)

D *Iris,* Siberian, 'Caesar's Brother' (3)

E *Allium cristophii.* Star of Persia (4)

F *Chrysanthemum maximum* 'Snowbank' or 'Snow Lady'. Shasta daisy (14)

G *Gypsophila paniculata* 'Perfecta'. Baby's breath (1)

H *Eupatorium coelestinum* 'Cori'. Hardy ageratum (4)

I *Geranium* 'Johnson's Blue'. Cranesbill (2)

J *Geranium himalayense* 'Plenum'. Cranesbill (5)

K *Nepeta × faassenii.* Catmint (5)

L *Aster amellus* 'Violet Queen'. Italian aster (7)

M *Veronica* 'Goodness Grows' (7)

N *Prunella grandiflora* 'Purple Loveliness'. Self-heal (6)

O *Dianthus* 'Aqua'. Pink (5)

P *Hosta* 'Francee'. Plantain lily (6)

SUMMERTIME BLUES If a big part of your summer involves trying to escape the heat, this cool collection should bring you at least the illusion of relief. From late spring through a midsummer crescendo until the last aster fades in fall, you'll be soothed by a continuous procession of blossoms in blue, purple, lavender, and white. Given regular moisture, all the plants will thrive in Zones 1–7, 32–43. An annual cleanup of the previous year's growth in late winter or early spring will ready the planting for a repeat performance.

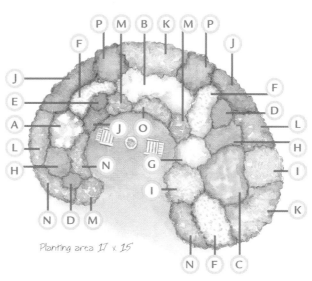

Planting area 17 x 15'

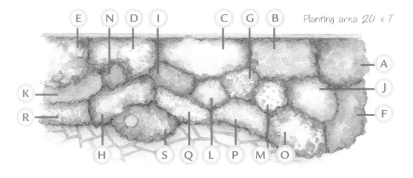

plant list

A *Salvia officinalis* 'Berggarten'. Common sage (1)

B *Malva moschata* 'Rosea'. Musk mallow (2)

C *Centranthus ruber* 'Albus'. Jupiter's beard (3)

D *Artemisia absinthium.* Common wormwood (2)

E *Lysimachia clethroides.* Gooseneck loosestrife (1)

F *Nepeta × faassenii.* Catmint (3)

G *Ruta graveolens* 'Jackman's Blue'. Rue (1)

H *Limonium platyphyllum.* Sea lavender (3)

I *Liatris spicata* 'Kobold'. Gayfeather (3)

J *Verbascum chaixii* 'Album'. Mullein (5)

K *Helictotrichon sempervirens.* Blue oat grass (2)

L *Iris,* tall bearded, 'Silverado' (2)

M *Hemerocallis,* cream cultivar. Daylily (1)

N *Allium aflatunense.* Ornamental allium (3)

O *Achillea clavennae.* Silvery yarrow (7)

P *Dianthus* 'Aqua'. Pink (6)

Q *Cerastium tomentosum.* Snow-in-summer (5)

R *Artemisia stelleriana* 'Silver Brocade'. Beach wormwood (3+)

S *Stachys byzantina* 'Silver Carpet'. Lamb's ears (7)

SILVER SETTING Cool, elegant, and restrained, this assemblage of gray, silver, white, ivory, lavender, and pink has an aura of refinement, a sophisticated shimmer that suggests the daytime equivalent of moonlight. Despite the quiet blend of colors, there's no lack of variety here; you'll note a range of plant shapes, leaf sizes, and foliage textures. Iris and allium bloom in spring, but most of the flowering plants put on their show in summer. This patrician pastiche is available to gardeners in much of the country: Zones 2–9, 14–24, 32–41.

Planting area 20' x 7'

plant list

A *Buddleja davidii* 'White Ball'.
Butterfly bush (1)

B *Rosa* 'Iceberg' (2)

C *Euonymus fortunei* 'Emerald Gaiety' (22)

D *Paeonia,* white cultivar. Peony (2)

E *Liatris scariosa* 'White Spire'.
Gayfeather (5)

F *Gypsophila paniculata* 'Perfecta'.
Baby's breath (3)

G *Chrysanthemum maximum*
'Aglaia'. Shasta daisy (9)

H *Achillea ptarmica* 'The Pearl'.
Yarrow (3)

I *Centranthus ruber* 'Albus'. Jupiter's beard (5)

J *Phlox maculata* 'Miss Lingard'. Thick-leaf phlox (5)

K *Iris,* Siberian, 'Fourfold White' (3)

L *Scabiosa caucasica* 'Alba'. Pincushion flower (3)

M *Campanula persicifolia,* white cultivar.
Peach-leafed bluebell (4)

N *Arrhenatherum elatius bulbosum*
'Variegatum'.
Bulbous oat grass (4)

O *Dianthus* 'Aqua'. Pink (4)

P *Prunella grandiflora*
'White Loveliness'.
Self-heal (7)

Q *Potentilla alba.*
Cinquefoil (5)

Planting area 14' x 15'

PEARLS AND JADE Plant habits and foliage textures are so varied you may not immediately realize that this plan includes just two colors: white and green. The plants suggested here all succeed in Zones 3–7, 32–34, 37, and 39. To extend the plan into Zones 35, 36, 38, 40, and 41, use a white cultivar of common lilac *(Syringa vulgaris)* in place of butterfly bush (A in the list at left). In Zones 8, 9, 10, and 14, replace oat grass (N) with lily turf *(Liriope muscari* 'Monroe White'); the lily turf may outperform oat grass in Zones 7, 32, and 33, as well.

floral ribbons

tom's notebook

This deliciously colorful flower border is situated between a lush green lawn and an impressive stand of blue-green conifers. The gardener started by building a berm of soil to add height to the composition, so even if all the plants were the same height, they appear taller in the center of the berm. This allows plants to be "stacked" for more visible color per square foot.

Drifts of gray-leafed plants like lamb's ears and artemisia serve as a unifying element, while also making the pastel hues appear brighter. (Silver and gray are also valuable for moderating vividly contrasting colors, such as orange and blue.) Deep-pink sweet Williams punctuate the border all along its length, and annual poppies strike a similar color note. Ornamental allium, clary sage, and aster each contribute a slightly different shade of purple. The pale yellow daylilies are an elegant choice; just think how different a bright orange variety would look.

Tom

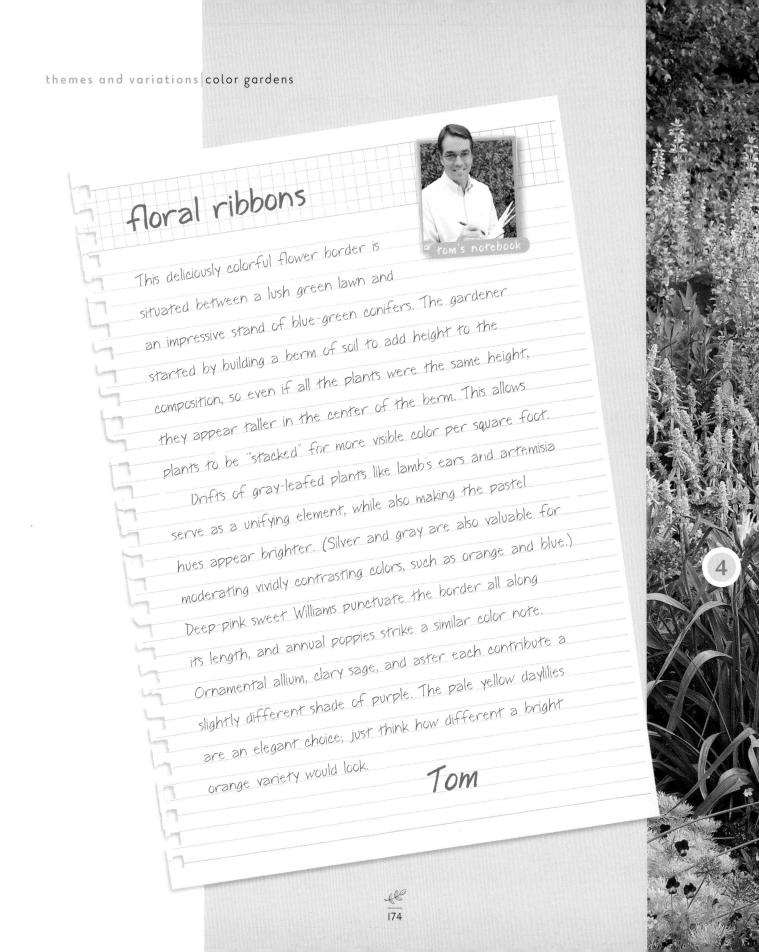

4

1 Leaves and seed pods are nearly as decorative as the poppy flowers

2 Sparkling white draws the eye to the end of the border

3 From the back porch, a giant wave of color appears to be crashing onto the lawn

4 Soft-hued daylilies won't be overlooked near the border's front

plant list

A *Lagerstroemia indica* 'Petite Snow'. Crape myrtle (1)

B *Lantana* 'Dwarf White' (1)

C *Lavandula × intermedia* 'White Spikes'. Lavandin (2)

D *Convolvulus cneorum.* Bush morning glory (1)

E *Artemisia arborescens* (1)

F *Ballota pseudodictamnus* (1)

G *Agapanthus* 'Rancho White'. Lily-of-the-Nile (4)

H *Iris,* tall bearded, 'Skating Party' or other white cultivar (3)

I *Penstemon* 'Holly's White'. Border penstemon (5)

J *Centranthus ruber* 'Albus'. Jupiter's beard (2)

K *Gazania,* white cultivar (4)

L *Achillea clavennae.* Silvery yarrow (4)

M *Stachys byzantina* 'Silver Carpet'. Lamb's ears (5)

N *Verbena pulchella gracilior* 'Alba'. Moss verbena (3)

Planting area 20 × 7.5

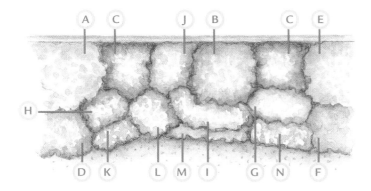

WHITEWASH Because many of the plants native to dry-summer, semiarid regions are gray foliaged, a white garden designed for such areas naturally becomes a symphony in white and silver. Carrying the silver banner in this planting are bush morning glory, artemisia, ballota, silvery yarrow, and lamb's ears. Blossoms—all of them in white, of course—begin in midspring with the bearded iris and continue through summer. This scheme flourishes in Zones 8, 9, 14, 18–21; with the simple substitution of *Nerium oleander* 'Morocco' for crape myrtle (A in the plant list), it will also succeed in Zones 15, 16, 22–24.

A GREEN TAPESTRY Green foliage takes center stage in this magnificent evergreen screen. The greens range from yellow-green to a deep, rich forest green, with accents of blue throughout. Although these are dwarf or small-growing varieties, excellent growing conditions over the years have caused the plants to grow together and upward toward the light, just as trees do in a forest. This Northwest garden can be replicated in Zones 4–6, 17, 32, 34, and 39.

Planting area 14' wide

plant list

A *Platycladus orientalis.* Oriental arborvitae (2)

B *Chamaecyparis obtusa* 'Nana Lutea'. Hinoki false cypress (1)

C *Juniperus squamata* 'Blue Star'. Juniper (1)

D *Tsuga canadensis* 'Gentsch White'. Canada hemlock (2)

E *Chamaecyparis obtusa* 'Nana Gracilis'. Hinoki false cypress (1)

F *Cryptomeria japonica* 'Elegans'. Plume cedar (1)

G *Chamaecyparis lawsoniana* 'Fletcher's White'. Port Orford cedar (1)

H *Picea pungens* 'Montgomery'. Colorado spruce (1)

I *Chamaecyparis pisifera* 'Golden Mops'. Sawara false cypress (1)

VACATIONING HOUSEPLANTS

Giving foliage houseplants a break from
being indoors will let them take on a new life
that will amaze you all summer and into the autumn. And if that snake
plant blooms in September, bring it back indoors during the evening
when it has a heavenly fragrance. Add a few annuals that are actually
tropicals for color, and you can create an outdoor garden for your
houseplants during the
warm weather in any
climate zone.

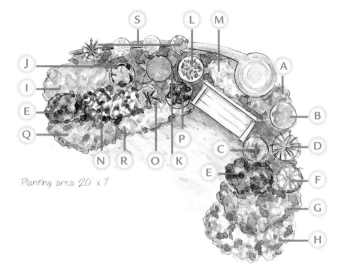

Planting area 20' x 7'

plant list

A *Philodendron scandens* (1)

B *Ficus elastica.* Rubber tree (1)

C *Cordyline fruticosa.* Ti plant (1)

D *Chamaedorea cataractarum.*
Cascade palm (1)

E *Solenostemon scutellarioides.* Coleus (2)

F *Dracaena fragrans.* Corn plant (1)

G *Begonia* (5)

H *Torenia fournieri.* Wishbone flower (12)

I *Schefflera arboricola.*
Hawaiian elf schefflera (1)

J *Dieffenbachia maculata.* Dumb cane (1)

K *Philodendron selloum* (1)

L *Araucaria heterophylla.*
Norfolk Island pine (1)

M *Epipremnum pinnatum* 'Aureum'.
Pothos (1)

N *Aphelandra squarrosa.* Zebra plant (1)

O *Sansevieria trifasciata.*
Bowstring hemp, snake plant (1)

P *Codiaeum variegatum* 'Pictum'.
Croton (1)

Q *Impatiens walleriana.* Busy Lizzie (18)

R *Tradescantia fluminensis.*
Wandering Jew (3)

S *Adiantum raddianum,* Maidenhair fern;
Chlorophytum comosum, Spider plant;
Aporocactus flagelliformis, Rat's tail
cactus; *Brassavola nodosa,* Lady of the
night (1 each)

plant list

A *Phormium* 'Maori Chief' (1)

B *Rosa* 'Charisma' (1)

C *Canna* 'Tropicanna' ('Phasion') or 'Pretoria' (3)

D *Felicia amelloides* 'San Gabriel' or 'San Luis'.
   Blue marguerite (1)

E *Penstemon* 'Firebird'. Border penstemon (3)

F *Ratibida columnifera.* Mexican hat (4)

G *Hemerocallis,* red cultivar. Daylily (3)

H *Hemerocallis,* orange cultivar. Daylily (4)

I *Hemerocallis* 'Stella de Oro'. Daylily (3)

J *Agapanthus* 'Storm Cloud'. Lily-of-the-Nile (2)

K *Coreopsis grandiflora* 'Early Sunrise' (7)

L *Coreopsis verticillata* 'Zagreb' (2)

M *Gaillardia* × *grandiflora* 'Goblin'. Blanket flower (7)

N *Osteospermum fruticosum* 'African Queen' or 'Burgundy'.
      Trailing African daisy (3)

       O *Verbena* 'Tapien Purple'. Moss verbena (8)

TROPIC TEMPO Neon-brilliant reds, oranges, and yellows are tempered with splashes of dark blue and purple in a tropical tapestry so vivid it virtually vibrates. Even the dominant foliage plants—canna and phormium—carry out the bright, hot theme. The planting is long and fairly narrow, suitable for a spot at the front of a garden or along a walkway, where it's certain to grab any passerby's attention. At its blazing best from late spring through summer, this assortment thrives in Zones 14–24.

Planting area 20' x 7'

HEAT WAVE Unabashedly hot, this lava-bright
combination of perennials and two annuals puts on
a summer-long show in Zones 1–9, 14–21, 31–43. The
dominant plant is the annual Mexican sunflower.
The other annual is that old favorite, French marigold—
much lower than the sunflower, but almost as striking
when massed in a tight circle to form a pool of glowing
color. Use the design as an island in a green lawn
or modify it to form a curving bed along a fence; just
divide it along the dotted line, then plant the larger half.

plant list

A *Rudbeckia fulgida sullivantii* 'Goldsturm' (3)

B *Achillea* 'Fireland'. Yarrow (2)

C *Achillea* 'Moonshine'. Yarrow (7)

D *Asclepias tuberosa*, Gay Butterflies strain. Butterfly weed (3)

E *Hemerocallis*, orange cultivar. Daylily (3)

F *Hemerocallis*, cream or light yellow cultivar. Daylily (2)

G *Hemerocallis* 'Black-eyed Stella'. Daylily (3)

H *Oenothera fruticosa* 'Fireworks' ('Fyrverkeri'). Sundrops (2)

I *Gaillardia* × *grandiflora* 'Tokajer'. Blanket flower (4)

J *Coreopsis auriculata* 'Nana' (4)

K *Potentilla atrosanguinea* 'Gibson's Scarlet'. Cinquefoil (6)

L *Tithonia rotundifolia*. Mexican sunflower (5)

M *Tagetes patula*. French marigold (10)

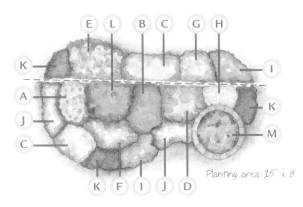

Planting area 15' x 8'

TROPICAL JEWELS You don't have to visit the tropics to enjoy jungly foliage and flowers. Just choose the right plants and you can have this tropical border in Zones 5–9, 12–31, H1, H2. You will need to plant this border for just one season in cold-winter areas, then start over the next year, or move the garden indoors for the winter. You can also substitute hardy look-alikes, such as Japanese banana *(Musa basjoo)* and honey bush *(Melianthus major)* for true tropicals. A pot filled with taro and sweet potato vine adds height and structure.

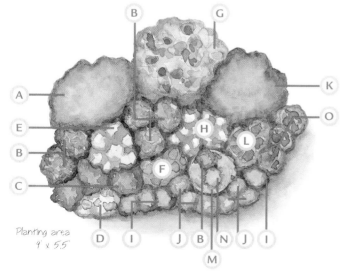

Planting area
9' x 5.5'

plant list

A *Phormium tenax.* New Zealand flax (1)

B *Asclepias curassavica* 'Silky Deep Red'. Blood flower (5)

C *Liriope muscari* 'Majestic'. Big blue lily turf (3)

D *Celosia,* assorted colors. Cockscomb (6)

E *Dahlia* 'Frau Louise Mayer' (5)

F *Dahlia* 'Park Record' (1)

G *Canna,* red and yellow cultivars (4)

H *Dahlia* 'Kevin Floodlight' (2)

I *Ophiopogon japonicus.* Mondo grass (4)

J *Zinnia elegans* 'Profusion Apricot' (6)

K *Strelitzia nicolai.* Giant bird of paradise (1)

L *Hibiscus rosa-sinensis* 'Brilliant'. Chinese hibiscus (1)

M *Ipomoea batatas* 'Marguerite'. Sweet potato vine (in pot) (1)

N *Colocasia esculenta* 'Ruffles'. Ruffled taro, elephant's ear (in pot) (1)

O *Anigozanthos* 'Kanga Red'. Kangaroo paw (3)

Perennials are a Northeast garden staple, as can be seen in this garden in full midsummer bloom. Periods of coolness and dormancy are essential for many of the most rewarding garden perennials, shrubs, and trees. Cool spring weather prolongs the blooming season of hardy bulbs and early-flowering perennials and annuals, while regular and abundant rains provide reliable precipitation throughout summer and fall.

sunset's climate zones

The key element to successful garden planning is choosing the right plants. As many gardeners have learned to their dismay, not every plant will do well in every garden.

When an unfamiliar plant strikes your fancy, you may have no trouble learning its basic needs: soil preference, water, and light. But a plant's performance is also governed by climate conditions, which include, in addition to winter lows and summer highs, length of the growing season, the timing and amount of rainfall, and overall humidity. While you can modify soil, apply or withhold water, or create shade to satisfy the needs of some plants, if the climate isn't right, they may fail despite your best efforts.

In this book, we assigned recommended climate zones for almost every plan, based on the Sunset climate zones, which are far more extensive than the familiar hardiness zone maps devised by the U.S. Department of Agriculture. Sunset's climate zone maps take all these plant performance factors into account rather than dividing the U.S. and Canada into broader zones based strictly on winter lows and record highs. The U.S.D.A. maps tell you only where a plant may survive the winter; our climate zone maps let you see where that plant will thrive year-round.

On pages 184–185 and 188–190 are brief descriptions of the zones illustrated on the maps on pages 186–187 and 190. For more information, consult Sunset's regional garden books.

A southwestern courtyard brims with vibrant color that can hold its own against the bright sunshine of a desert climate.

ZONE 1 | Coldest Winter Areas in the West

Growing season: mid-June to early Sept. in colder areas, mid-May to late Sept. in warmer areas. Average lows to 12° to 0°F/–12° to –18°C, extreme lows to –50°F/–46°C; snow cover (or winter mulch) key to perennials' success.

ZONE 2 | Second Coldest Western Climate

Growing season: mid-May to mid- to late Sept. Occurs at lower elevation than Zone 1; summers are mild to hot, winters to 10°F/–12°C (extremes to –20° to –30°F/–29° to –34°C) with snow. The coldest zone for growing sweet cherries, hardiest apples. Premier fruit- and grain-growing climate in locations with long, warm to hot summers.

ZONE 3 | Mildest Areas of High Elevations and Interior Climates

Growing season: mid-April to mid-Oct. Long, dry, warm summers favor a variety of warm-season crops, deciduous fruits, many ornamentals. Occurs at higher elevation the farther south it is found. Winter temperatures drop to 19° to 15°F/–7 ° to –9°C with extremes to –18°F/–28°C; snow is possible.

ZONE 4 | Cold-winter Western Washington, British Columbia, and Southern Alaska

Growing season: early May to early Oct. Summers are cool, thanks to ocean influence; chilly winters (34° to 28°F/1° to –20°C) result from elevation, influence of continental air mass, or both. Coolness, ample rain suit many perennials and bulbs.

ZONE 5 | Ocean-influenced Northwest Coast, Puget Sound, and Vancouver Island

Growing season: April to early Nov., typically with cool temperatures throughout. Less rain falls here than in Zone 4; January lows average 41° to 33°F (5° to 1°C), with annual lows a few degrees lower and 10-year extremes ranging from 20° to 6°F/–7° to –14°C. This "English garden" climate is ideal for rhododendrons and many rock garden plants.

ZONE 6 | The Willamette and Columbia River Valleys

Growing season: mid-Mar. to mid-Nov., with somewhat warmer temperatures than in Zone 5. Ocean influence keeps winter lows about the same as in Zone 5. Climate suits all but tender plants and those needing hot or dry summers.

ZONE 7 | Oregon's Rogue River Valley, California's High Foothills

Growing season: May to early Oct. Summers are hot and dry; typical winter lows run from 35° to 26°F/–2° to –3°C. The summer-winter contrast suits plants that need dry, hot summers and moist, only moderately cold winters.

ZONE 8 | Cold-air Basins of California's Central Valley

Growing season: mid-Feb. through Nov. This is a valley floor with no maritime influence. Summers are hot; winter lows range from 29° to 13°F/–2° to –11°C. Rain comes in the cooler months, covering just the early part of the growing season.

ZONE 9 | Thermal Belts of California's Central Valley

Growing season: late Feb. through Nov. Zone 9 is located in the higher elevations around Zone 8, but its summers are just as hot; its winter lows are slightly higher (temperatures range from 28° to 18°F/–2° to –8°C). Rainfall pattern is the same as in Zone 8.

ZONE 10 | High Desert Areas of Arizona, New Mexico, West Texas, Oklahoma Panhandle, and Southwest Kansas

Growing season: early April to early Nov. Chilly (even snow-dusted) weather rules from late Nov. through Feb., with lows from 32° to 23°F/0° to –5°C. Rain comes in summer as well as in the cooler seasons.

ZONE 11 | Medium to High Desert of California and Southern Nevada

Growing season: late March to early Nov. Summers are sizzling, with 110 days above 90°F/32°C. Balancing this is a 3½-month winter, with 85 nights below freezing and lows from 11° to 0°F/–12° to –18°C. Scant rainfall comes in winter.

ZONE 12 | Arizona's Intermediate Desert

Growing season: mid-Mar. to late Nov., with scorching midsummer heat. Compared with Zone 13, this region has harder frosts; record low is 6°F/–14°C. Rains come in summer and winter.

ZONE 13 | Low or Subtropical Desert

Growing season: mid-Feb. through Nov., interrupted by nearly 3 months of incandescent, growth-stopping summer heat. Most frosts are light (record lows run from 27° to 15°F/–3° to –9°C); scant rain comes in summer and winter.

ZONE 14 | Inland Northern and Central California with Some Ocean Influence

Growing season: early Mar. to mid-Nov., with rain coming in the remaining months. Periodic intrusions of marine air temper summer heat and winter cold (lows run from 26° to 16°F/ –3° to –9°C). Mediterranean-climate plants are at home here.

ZONE 15 | Northern and Central California's Chilly-winter Coast-influenced Areas

Growing season: Mar. to Nov. Rain comes from fall through winter. Typical winter lows range from 28° to 21°F/–2° to –6°C. Maritime air influences the zone much of the time, giving it cooler, moister summers than Zone 14.

ZONE 16 | Northern and Central California Coast Range Thermal Belts

Growing season: late Feb. to late Nov. With cold air draining to lower elevations, winter lows typically run from 32° to 19°F/0° to –7°C. Like Zone 15, this region is dominated by maritime air, but its winters are milder on average.

ZONE 17 | Oceanside Northern and Central California and Southernmost Oregon

Growing season: late Feb. to late Nov.. Coolness and fog are hallmarks; summer highs seldom top 75°F/24°C, while winter lows run from 36° to 23°F/2° to –5°C. Heat-loving plants disappoint or dwindle here.

ZONE 18 | Hilltops and Valley Floors of Interior Southern California

Growing season: mid-Mar. through late Nov. Summers are hot and dry; rain comes in winter, when lows reach 22° to 17°F/–6° to –8°C. Plants from the Mediterranean and Near Eastern regions thrive here.

ZONE 19 | Thermal Belts around Southern California's Interior Valleys

Growing season: early Mar. to early Dec. As in Zone 18, rainy winters and hot, dry summers are the norm—but here, winter lows dip only to 28° to 22°F/–2° to –6°C, allowing some tender evergreen plants to grow outdoors with protection.

ZONE 20 | Hilltops and Valley Floors of Ocean-influenced Inland Southern California

Growing season: late Mar. to late Nov.—but fairly mild winters (typical lows of 43° to 37° F/6° to 3°C) allow gardening through much of the year. Cool and moist maritime influence alternates with hot, dry interior air.

ZONE 21 | Thermal Belts around Southern California's Ocean-influenced Interior Valleys

Growing season: early Mar. to early Dec., with same tradeoff of oceanic and interior influence as in Zone 20. During winter rainy season, lows rarely drop below 30°F (–1°C) with extremes to 25° F (–4°C).

ZONE 22 | Colder-winter Parts of Southern California's Coastal Region

Growing season: Mar. to early Dec. Winter lows seldom fall below 28° to 25°F/–2° to –9°C, though colder air sinks to this zone from Zone 23. Summers are warm; rain comes in winter. Climate here is largely oceanic.

ZONE 23 | Thermal Belts of Southern California's Coastal Region

Growing season: almost year-round (all but first half of Jan.). Rain comes in winter. Reliable ocean influence keeps summers

descriptions continue, page 188 >

Climate Zones | / | 1 | 2 | 3 | 4 | 5 | 6 | 7 | 8 | 9 | 10 | 11 | 12 | 13 | 14 | 15 | 16 | 17 | 18 | 19 | 20 | 21 | 22 | 23 | 24 | 25 | 26 | 27 | 28

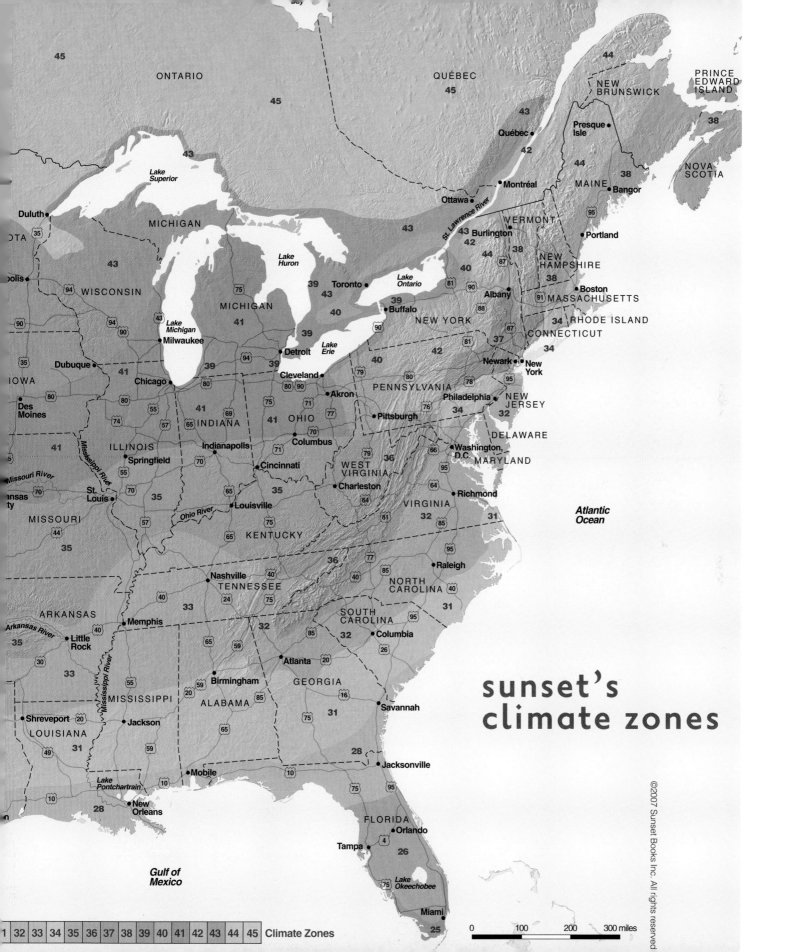

ONTARIO

QUÉBEC
45

45

PRINCE
EDWARD
ISLAND

NEW
BRUNSWICK

44

45

NOVA
SCOTIA

38

43

42

Presque
Isle

Québec

Montréal

*Lake
Superior*

43

MAINE

Bangor

38

44

Duluth

35

Ottawa

St. Lawrence River

VERMONT

43

Portland

38

MICHIGAN

43

NEW
HAMPSHIRE

Burlington

42

87

44

38

…OTA

43

*Lake
Huron*

39

Toronto

*Lake
Ontario*

43

81

40

44

87

Albany

88

38

Boston

…olis

94

WISCONSIN

MICHIGAN

75

90

91

MASSACHUSETTS

43

*Lake
Michigan*

41

39

40

Buffalo

NEW YORK

34

RHODE ISLAND

90

43

90

39

*Lake
Erie*

750

87

CONNECTICUT

34

Milwaukee

94

42

81

37

94

39

Detroit

40

79

80

Newark

95

New
York

34

Dubuque

41

Chicago

80

Cleveland

80 90

PENNSYLVANIA

78

32

IOWA

90

80

55

Akron

71

Philadelphia

NEW
JERSEY

35

Des
Moines

74

57

69

41

OHIO

77

76

34

DELAWARE

65

INDIANA

70

Columbus

66

95

41

ILLINOIS

Indianapolis

71

Pittsburgh

Washington,
D.C.

Springfield

70

Cincinnati

79

MARYLAND

Missouri River

55

WEST
VIRGINIA

36

95

Mississippi River

65

35

Charleston

64

Richmond

St.
Louis

70

Louisville

64

VIRGINIA

…ansas
ty

70

Ohio River

57

81

32

31

MISSOURI

65

KENTUCKY

85

44

95

35

36

77

Raleigh

40

33

Nashville

540

TENNESSEE

710

85

NORTH
CAROLINA

40

ARKARSAS

40

24

75

31

Arkansas River

Memphis

35

32

SOUTH
CAROLINA

95

Little
Rock

40

65

59

85

32

Columbia

30

33

85

26

Atlanta

20

55

59

Birmingham

Mississippi River

20

GEORGIA

16

MISSISSIPPI

ALABAMA

85

31

Savannah

Shreveport

20

Jackson

65

75

LOUISIANA

31

59

28

49

Jacksonville

10

Mobile

10

75

95

10

*Lake
Pontchartrain*

28

New
Orleans

FLORIDA

Orlando

4

*Gulf of
Mexico*

Tampa

26

75

*Lake
Okeechobee*

Miami

25

*Atlantic
Ocean*

sunset's
climate zones

0   100   200   300 miles

| 1 | 32 | 33 | 34 | 35 | 36 | 37 | 38 | 39 | 40 | 41 | 42 | 43 | 44 | 45 | **Climate Zones** |

mild (except when hot Santa Ana winds come from inland), frosts negligible; average lows range from 48° to 43°F/9° to 6°C; extreme lows average 34° to 27°F/1° to 3°C.

ZONE 24 | Marine-dominated Southern California Coast
Growing season: all year, but periodic freezes have dramatic effects. Winter lows average 48° to 42° F/9° to 5° C, with all-time lows at about 20° F/–6° C. Climate here is oceanic (but warmer than oceanic Zone 17), with cool summers, mild winters. Record heat is usually in October. Subtropical plants thrive.

ZONE 25 | South Florida and the Keys
Growing season: all year. Add ample year-round rainfall (least in Dec. through Mar.), high humidity, and overall warmth, and you have a near-tropical climate. The Keys are frost-free; winter lows elsewhere run from 40° to 25°F/4° to –4°C.

ZONE 26 | Central and Interior Florida
Growing season: early Feb. to late Dec., with typically humid, warm to hot weather. Rain is plentiful all year, heaviest in summer and early fall. Lows range from 15°F/–9°C in the north to 27°F/–3°C in the south; arctic air brings periodic hard freezes.

ZONE 27 | Lower Rio Grande Valley
Growing season: early Mar. to mid-Dec. Summers are hot and humid; winter lows only rarely dip below freezing. Many plants from tropical and subtropical Africa and South America are well adapted here.

ZONE 28 | Gulf Coast, North Florida, Atlantic Coast to Charleston
Growing season: mid-Mar. to early Dec. Humidity and rainfall are year-round phenomena; summers are hot, winters virtually frostless but subject to periodic invasions by frigid arctic air. Azaleas, camellias, many subtropicals flourish.

ZONE 29 | Interior Plains of South Texas
Growing season: mid-Mar. through Nov. Moderate rainfall (to 25 inches annually) comes year-round. Summers are hot. Winter lows can dip to 26°F/–3°C, with occasional arctic freezes bringing much lower readings.

ZONE 30 | Hill Country of Central Texas
Growing season: mid-Mar. through Nov. Zone 30 has higher annual rainfall than Zone 29 (to 35 inches) and lower winter temperatures, normally to around 20°F/–7°C. Seasonal variations favor many fruit crops, perennials.

ZONE 31 | Interior Plains of Gulf Coast and Coastal Southeast
Growing season: mid-Mar. to early Nov. In this extensive east-west zone, hot and sticky summers contrast with chilly winters (record low temperatures are 7° to 0°F/–14° to –18°C). There's rain all year (an annual average of 50 inches), with the least falling in Oct.

ZONE 32 | Interior Plains of Mid-Atlantic States; Chesapeake Bay, Southeastern Pennsylvania, Southern New Jersey
Growing season: late Mar. to early Nov. Rain falls year-round (40 inches to 50 inches annually); winter lows (moving through the zone from south to north) are 30° to 20°F/–1° to –7°C. Humidity is less oppressive here than in Zone 31.

ZONE 33 | North-Central Texas and Oklahoma Eastward to the Appalachian Foothills
Growing season: mid-April through Oct. Warm Gulf Coast air and colder continental/arctic fronts both play a role; their unpredictable interplay results in a wide range in annual rainfall (22 inches to 52 inches) and winter lows (20° to 0°F/–7° to –18°C). Summers are muggy and warm to hot.

ZONE 34 | Lowlands and Coast from Gettysburg to North of Boston
Growing season: late April to late Oct. Ample rainfall and humid summers are the norm. Winters are variable—typically fairly mild (around 20°F/–7°C), but with lows down to –3° to –22°F/–19° to –30°C if arctic air swoops in.

ZONE 35 | Ouachita Mountains, Northern Oklahoma and Arkansas, Southern Kansas to North-Central Kentucky and Southern Ohio

Growing season: late April to late Oct. Rain comes in all seasons. Summers can be truly hot and humid. Without arctic fronts, winter lows are around 18°F/–8°C; with them, the coldest weather may bring lows of –20°F/–29°C.

ZONE 36 | Appalachian Mountains

Growing season: May to late Oct. Thanks to greater elevation, summers are cooler and less humid, winters colder (0° to –20°F/–18° to –29°C) than in adjacent, lower zones. Rain comes all year (heaviest in spring). Late frosts are common.

ZONE 37 | Hudson Valley and Appalachian Plateau

Growing season: May to mid-Oct., with rainfall throughout. Lower in elevation than neighboring Zone 42, with warmer winters: lows are 0° to –5°F/–18° to –21°C, unless arctic air moves in. Summer is warm to hot, humid.

ZONE 38 | New England Interior and Lowland Maine

Growing season: May to early Oct. Summers feature reliable rainfall and lack oppressive humidity of lower-elevation, more southerly areas. Winter lows dip to –10° to –20°F/–23° to –29°C , with periodic colder temperatures due to influxes of arctic air.

ZONE 39 | Shoreline Regions of the Great Lakes

Growing season: early May to early Oct. Springs and summers are cooler here, autumns milder than in areas farther from the lakes. Southeast lakeshores get the heaviest snowfalls. Lows reach 0° to –10°F/–18° to –23°C.

ZONE 40 | Inland Plains of Lake Erie and Lake Ontario

Growing season: mid-May to mid-Sept., with rainy, warm, variably humid weather. The lakes help moderate winter lows; temperatures typically range from –10° to –20°F/–23° to –29°C, with occasional colder readings when arctic fronts rush through.

ZONE 41 | Northeast Kansas and Southeast Nebraska to Northern Illinois and Indiana, Southeast Wisconsin, Michigan, Northern Ohio

Growing season: early May to early Oct. Winter brings average lows of –11° to –20°F/–23° to –29°C. Summers in this zone are hotter and longer west of the Mississippi, cooler and shorter nearer the Great Lakes; summer rainfall increases in the same west-to-east direction.

ZONE 42 | Interior Pennsylvania and New York; St. Lawrence Valley

Growing season: late May to late Sept. This zone's elevation gives it colder winters than surrounding zones: lows range from –20° to –40°F/–29° to –40°C, with the colder readings coming in the Canadian portion of the zone. Summers are humid, rainy.

ZONE 43 | Upper Mississippi Valley, Upper Michigan, Southern Ontario and Quebec

Growing season: late May to mid-Sept. The climate is humid from spring through early fall; summer rains are usually dependable. Arctic air dominates in winter, with lows typically from –20° to –30°F/–29° to –34°C.

ZONE 44 | Mountains of New England and Southeastern Quebec

Growing season: June to mid-Sept. Latitude and elevation give fairly cool, rainy summers, cold winters with lows of –20° to –40°F/–29° to –40°C. Choose short-season, low heat-requirement annuals and vegetables.

ZONE 45 | Northern Parts of Minnesota and Wisconsin, Eastern Manitoba through Interior Quebec

Growing season: mid-June through Aug., with rain throughout; rainfall (and humidity) are least in zone's western part, greatest in eastern reaches. Winters are frigid (–30° to –40°F/–34° to –40°C), with snow cover, deeply frozen soil.

descriptions continue >

ZONE A1 | Alaska's Coldest Climate—Fairbanks and the Interior

Growing season: mid-May to early Sept. Summer days are long, mild to warm; permafrost usually recedes below root zone. Winter offers reliable snow cover. Season extenders include planting in south and west exposures, boosting soil temperature with mulches or IRT plastic sheeting. Winter lows drop to –10° to –20°F/–23° to –29°C, with occasional extremes to –60°F/–51°C.

ZONE A2 | The Intermediate Climate of Anchorage and Cook Inlet

Growing season: mid-May to mid-Sept. Climate is moderated by mountains to the north and south, also by water of Cook Inlet. Microclimates reign supreme: winter lows may be 6° to 0°F/–14° to –18°C but with extremes of –20° to –30°F/–29° to –34°C possible. Summer days are cool to mild and frequently cloudy.

ZONE A3 | Mild Southern Maritime Climate from Kodiak to Juneau

Growing season: mid-May to late Sept. Summers are cool and cloudy, winters rainy and windy. Typical lows are to 20° to 30°F/–7° to –1°C with extremes to –5°F/–21°C. Winter-spring freeze-thaw cycles damage plants that break growth early. Cool-weather plants revel in climate but annual types mature more slowly than usual.

ZONE H1 | Cooler Volcanic Slopes from 2,000 to 5,000 Feet

Found only on Hawaii and Maui, this zone offers cooler air (and cooler nights) than lower Zone H2; temperatures here are better for low-chill fruits (especially at higher elevations) and many nontropical ornamentals. Warm-season highs reach 65° to 80°F/19° to 27°C; cool-season lows drop to around 45°F/7°C.

ZONE H2 | Sea Level to 2,000 Feet: the Coconut Palm Belt

The most heavily populated region in the islands, this has a tepid climate with high temperatures in the 80° to 90°F/27° to 32°C range, low temperatures only to about 65°F/18°C. Rainiest period is Nov. through March, the remaining months, on leeward sides, being relatively dry. Windward sides of islands get more precipitation than leeward sides from passing storms and year-round tradewind showers.

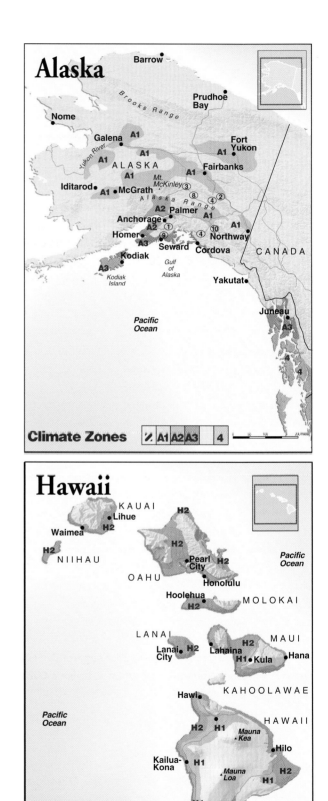

designers

Maile Arnold: 118 bottom, 134; **Pamela Baggett, Singing Springs Nursery**: 178; **Shari Bashin-Sullivan, Design; Enchanted Planting, Plantings**: 118 top left, 126–127; **David C. Becker**: 118 top middle left, 162; **Susan Blevins**: 183; **Greg Bobich, Designs by Sundown**: 62–63; Julie Chai: 108; **Jess Chamberlain and Ryan Casey**: 118 top right, 146; Bob Clark: 66, 170; **Cleaver Design Associates, Design; Enchanting Planting, Plantings**: 4; Linda Cochran: 8 top center right, 80; **Robert Cornell & Associates**: 61; Karen Donnelly: 181; **Phil Edinger**: 3 bottom left, 9, 13, 14, 15, 17, 18, 19, 20, 21, 24, 25, 28, 29, 35, 36, 42, 43, 49, 53, 56, 57, 64, 65, 67, 69, 70, 71, 73, 75, 78 top, 79 top, 85, 86, 93, 94, 96–97, 98, 100, 101, 109, 113, 114, 115, 118 top middle right, 119, 123, 124, 125, 130, 131, 132–135, 136, 137, 147, 148, 152, 153, 154–155, 158, 159, 160, 161, 163, 166, 167, 171, 172, 173, 176, 179, 180; **David Felix**: 2 left, 32; **Sharon Finkle**: 82; **Gay Bonorden Gray**: 86; Donna Hackman: 48; **Jack Hagenaars & Keith Webb**: 120; **Heather Hardcaste, Breaking Ground Landscape Design**: 99; **Lucy I. Hardiman, Perennial Partners**: 34; **Ralph Hastings and Holly Turner**: 177; **Randall Holman**: 91; Michael Hopping: 117; **Kristin Horne**: 3 bottom right, 182; **Raymond Jungles**: 142; **Judy Kameon, Elysian Landscapes**: 90; Allen Thomas Koster: 11; **Rick La Frentz**: 140, 143; **Tom Mannion**: 76–77; **Phyllis McMorrow**: 47, 169; **David McMullin, New Moon Gardens**: 168; **Samantha Dardick Mier and Joel Mier in collaboration with Jon Buerk, J. Buerk Landscape/ Maintenance**: 58–59; **Valerie Murray**: 89; **Natural Garden by Carole Kraft**: 74; **Gary Patterson**: 95, 149, 165; Joanna Reed: 157; **Chris Rosmini Landscape Design**: 46; **R. Michael Schneider, Orange Street Studio**: 5, 31; **Steven Schram, Island Gardens Company**: 102; Jeanie C. Sims: 16; **Jill Slater**: 12, 44–45; **Jill Stenn, Stenn Design**: 8 bottom, 51; **Bud Stuckey**: 52, 156; **Freeland and Sabrina Tanner, Proscape Landscape Design**: 3 top, 8 top left, 33, 84, 118 bottom, 150–151; **Betty Taylor**: 175; **Jeffrey Trent**: 39; **Truxell & Valentino Landscape Developers**: 26; **Margaret de Haas van Dorsser**: 60; **Jeni Webber**: 6; **Lew Whitney, Roger's Gardens**: 72; **Judy Wigand**: 92; **Tom Wilhite**: 1, 22–23, 27, 37, 40, 55, 87, 104–105, 112, 122, 128–129; **Nick Williams**: 106–107

photographers

Carolyn L. Bates Photography: 11; **Paul Bousquet**: 16, 62; **Marion Brenner**: 8 top left, 10, 12, 22, 23, 27, 40, 44, 45, 55, 66, 84 left, 104, 105, 112, 170; **Rob D. Brodman**: 58, 59, 68, 82 left and right, 118 top right, 146, 164, 181; **Alan & Linda Detrick**: 84 right; **Andrew Drake**: 8 bottom, 51; **Laura Dunkin-Hubby**: 8 top right, 107 bottom right; **Roger Foley**: 48, 76, 77, 142, 157; **Frank Gaglione**: 91, 99; **David Goldberg**: 129; **Steven Gunther**: 5, 31, 46, 61, 72 top left, 90; **Paul Hammond**: 72 right; **Jerry Harpur/Harpur Garden Images**: 144; **Saxon Holt**: 3 top, 118 top left and bottom, 126, 127, 134, 150, 151; **N. D. Koster Photographics**: 30, 38, 54, 88, 116, 138, 174; **Janet Loughrey Photography**: 8 top middle right, 34, 60, 80; **Allan Mandell**: 120; **Charles Mann**: 183; **Terrence Moore**: 39; **Jerry Pavia**: 33, 47, 102, 121, 169; **Norman A. Plate**: 92, 156; **Norm Plate**: 2 right, 4, 89, 139, 175, 177; **Susan A. Roth**: 3 bottom right, 182; **SPC Photo Collection**: 117; **Thomas J. Story**: 52, 74, 86, 108, 118 top middle left, 122, 128 top, 145, 162; **Michael S. Thompson**: 82 middle; **E. Spencer Toy**: 107 bottom left; **Lee Anne White**: 2 left, 6, 32, 168; **Tom Woodward**: 71, 106, 128 bottom

illustrators

Gwendolyn Babbitt: 9, 73, 75, 78 top, 85, 119, , 131, 132, 154, 171, 172, 173, 176; **Pamela Baggett**: 178; **Marcie Hawthorne**: 17, 19, 100, 101, 136, 137. 166; **Lois Lovejoy**: 18, 24, 25, 95, 96, 98, 109, 113, 130, 140, 143, 149, 163, 165; **Erin O'Toole**: 14, 15, 26, 28, 29, 35, 36, 42, 43, 49, 53, 56, 57, 67, 69, 70, 71, 93, 123, 124, 125, 135, 152, 153, 167, 180; **Mark Pechenik**: 41, 103, 106, 110; **Elayne Sears**: 13, 20, 21 64, 65, 83, 94, 147, 148; **Jenny Speckels**: 1, 7, 8 top middle left, 37, 78 bottom, 81, 87, 114, 115, 118 top middle right, 141, 158, 159, 160, 161, 179

Plot plans: **Jenny Speckels**
Additional plot plans: **Mark Pechenik**: 41, 103, 107, 111; **Beverley Bozarth Colgan**: 112, 122, 129; **Pamela Baggett**: 178

acknowledgments *Numerous writers, editors, and designers contributed to this book. In particular, Phil Edinger deserves a big thank you for his work on this book's predecessor,* Garden Designs. *We would also like to thank Philip Thornburg for his help.*

index